Lucid relevance meeting truth. Terry gi[v]
theological insight with a Skin Bracer w
over, Starbucks!

—GREG BALL, SENIOR PASTOR
MORNING STAR, AUSTIN, TEXAS
PRESIDENT, CHAMPIONS FOR CHRIST

As a family physician I appreciate how important it is to my patients' health for them to be aware of the God-given purpose for their lives. Destiny and purpose are to the spirit of man as micronutrients are to the body. Unfortunately, the discipline of medicine has largely been practiced in separation from a patient's spirituality. In his new book, *Awakened to Destiny*, Terry Crist shows us the importance of discovering our own individual destiny and its role in our spiritual condition. This book provides the blueprints for building a life of greatness.

—ROBERT T. BAILEY, PHARM.D., M.D.
ASSOCIATE PROFESSOR OF FAMILY MEDICINE
FAMILY PHYSICIAN, SCOTTSDALE, ARIZONA

I am glad to know that Terry has written again. His perspective is immensely refreshing and deeply needed. Hope arises in the human heart when we see the God-ordained destiny that Terry proclaims. *Awakened to Destiny* is sure to change the lives of many.

—DUDLEY HALL, FOUNDER AND PRESIDENT
SUCCESSFUL CHRISTIAN LIVING MINISTRIES

Terry Crist's passion is to awaken the narcoleptic, saved and unsaved, to the amazing life God has for the elect this side of the Judgment Seat. The secularization of the Western world has effectively removed a Designer and thus a design from the mind of postmodern man, leaving this generation more lost than Britney Spears at a Vaclav Havel read. Terry knows the landscape of the human condition. He has accumulated wisdom from some of our world's greatest minds, and most importantly, he has tackled the topic of destiny within a proper theological framework. *Awakened to Destiny* will be a shot of spiritual espresso to the thoughtful reader.

—DOUG GILES, SENIOR PASTOR
HIS PEOPLE CHRISTIAN CHURCH, MIAMI, FLORIDA
AUTHOR AND BROADCASTER

Awakened to Destiny reminds us that true success is being devoted at every level of life until we hear Jesus proclaim, "Well done, thou good and faithful servant." Thank you, son, for awakening us to the importance of continually aligning our lives with the purposes of God.

—T. MICHAEL CRIST SR., SENIOR PASTOR
GEORGETOWN PENTECOSTAL CHURCH, GEORGETOWN, LOUISIANA

Terry Crist will help any reader move out of the fog and into the light of destiny. Serious about discovering God's destiny for life? Immediately read and implement the journey described so clearly in this essential book for spiritual growth.

—DR. LARRY KEEFAUVER
SENIOR EDITORIAL ADVISER, *MINISTRIES TODAY*
BEST-SELLING AUTHOR

Ours is a schizophrenic generation floundering in tortured inner confusion between a self-destructive drivenness and a meandering, shuffling pointlessness. Terry Crist beckons the suburban workaholic to find significance beyond function. He likewise confronts lobotomized wretches ambling through life with amiable purposelessness. His voice is that of a spiritual alarm clock. Awake, thou that sleepest!

—DR. MARK RUTLAND, PRESIDENT
SOUTHEASTERN COLLEGE, LAKELAND, FLORIDA

There is a reason—a very big reason—why God sovereignly chose you to be part of the inaugural generation of the Third Millenium. Terry Crist's book could not be timelier. Lucid and cogent, this book is literally a prophetic wake-up call. Your dormant dreams are about to be resurrected. *Awakened to Destiny* is a "must-read" for those who intuitively know that they are meant for something more and that a grand design has birthed them onto history's stage "for such a time as this."

—DAVID SHIBLEY
PRESIDENT, GLOBAL ADVANCE

AWAKENED TO
DESTINY

Charisma®
HOUSE
Books about Spirit-Led Living

TERRY CRIST

AWAKENED TO DESTINY by Terry Crist
Published by Charisma House
A part of Strang Communications Company
600 Rinehart Road
Lake Mary, Florida 32746
www.charismahouse.com

Unless otherwise noted, all Scripture quotations are from the New King James Version of the Bible. Copyright ©1979, 1980, 1982 by Thomas Nelson, Inc., publishers. Used by permission.

Scripture quotations marked KJV are from the King James Version of the Bible.

Scripture quotations marked NAS are from the New American Standard Bible. Copyright © 1960, 1962, 1963, 1968, 1971, 1972, 1973, 1975, 1977 by the Lockman Foundation. Used by permission. (www.Lockman.org)

Scripture quotations marked NIV are from the Holy Bible, New International Version. Copyright © 1973, 1978, 1984, International Bible Society. Used by permission.

Scripture quotations marked THE MESSAGE are from THE MESSAGE. Copyright © 1993, 1994, 1995. Used by permission of NavPress Publishing Group.

Incidents and persons portrayed in this volume are based on fact. However, some names and details have been changed to protect the privacy of individuals.

Cover design by Rachel Campbell

Library of Congress Catalog Card Number: 2002103066
International Standard Book Number: 0-88419-770-0

02 03 04 05   8 7 6 5 4 3 2 1
Printed in the United States of America

This book is dedicated to my youngest son, Tyler. Your enthusiasm for life has forever changed my world. The future is ours— together.

Acknowledgments

Let's get one thing clear from the beginning—this book is stolen property. It is the collection of lessons that I've learned over the years from great leaders who were willing to invest into the development of my potential. Long ago I gave up the indignity of having to admit that my life is the sum of what others have taught me. I am happy to acknowledge their involvement. The problem is, there are so many people to thank I know not where to begin...or end. Let me highlight a couple of names that deserve special mention.

First, I want to express my appreciation to my parents for teaching me to believe that my life was destined for greatness. Although I still wrestle with my doubts, the point was well taken. Early in life, their relentless faith in my budding ability positioned me to take unusual risks and to experience exceptional results.

To the pastors who allow me the privilege of coaching them into greatness, you are the reason I spring out of bed each morning.

Thank you to the Charisma House publishing team—David Welday for believing in this message and convincing me that it was important enough to write, Barbara Dycus for fine-tuning my grammar and bolstering my confidence.

Special thanks to Alan Nelson for befriending me—on and off the basketball court. The foreword lends credibility to this humble author.

Finally, my deepest gratitude to the greatest family one could possibly ever have: Judith, Mickey, Joshie, Tybo and Bubby. I love you, guys!

Suffice it to say, this book is the test I am taking on the lessons I have been taught on destiny. I hope I've gotten the answers right.

Contents

Section I
The Awakening

Section II
The Discovery

Section III
The Journey

Foreword

My friend and mentor Dr. Leslie Parrott told me about hearing the famed Swiss psychologist Paul Tournier. Dr. Tournier, author of *The Meaning of Persons*, talked about the human need for people to find "a place." Everyone has a place in life where you feel at home. The place may be geographical, but it tends to be more of purpose—a meshing of task/role/relationships with calling. All of us have an inner voice that beckons us to discover and align ourselves with this place. When we're in our place, there is compatibility within ourselves as well as with others. When we're not in our place, it makes others uncomfortable as well. If you walk into a place and someone says, "What are you doing here?", it may be a sign that others sense that you are out of your place.

So how do you find your place, your destiny, your niche in life?

I've read two good books on the subject of discovering your destiny: *Finding Your Mission* by Richard Bolles and the one you're now holding. "Destiny is more than a conscious awareness of the destination. It is the lifelong journey toward the destination." These are the words of Terry Crist, ideas that provide keen insight into the elusive realm of personal destiny. Like Terry, I too have sensed a divine sense of destiny for most of my life. When I was a young adult, I used to ask people the question, "What are your dreams?" After awhile, my wife lovingly reproved me. She said, "Don't ask people that question. It's too intimidating. You have dreams and a sense of destiny, but most people do not." Over the years I've discovered, as in most things, that my wife is right. Most people do not have a strong sense of destiny in their lives.

It is not easy to talk about destiny. During Midwest winters as a child, I used to watch my breath vaporize as I exhaled. As kids we pretended we were smoking, feigning fake cigarettes.

The tiny clouds whirled upward and then disappeared. Trying to put your arms around a concept like destiny is akin to grabbing one of those breath vapors. Believe it or not, Terry helps us do that, placing handles on the concept so that we can hold on to it and even take it with us. I applaud both his daring to address such a vital but nebulous topic, as well as his energy in discussing the matter. Destiny and destination share the same etymology. The main difference is that in the destiny, the journey is the destination.

Whether it is Queen Esther discovering the purpose of her life for a specific moment in history or Moses who invested decades in leading God's people, our "place" is vital to us as well as others. The only problem with using renowned people as examples is that they tend to intimidate us into thinking we're not valuable if our calling is not some grand, famous role. That perception is unfounded. You cannot compare callings. Each person's is equal so long as it is God-given and pursued with passion and vigilance. That is where books like this become so important, because the task of discovering our individual destiny is so vital.

While the intangible subject of destiny might seem a philosopher's delight, Terry provides an array of quotes, stories and illustrations that make his points memorable and user-friendly. Throughout the pages, you realize that you are not the only one who has wrestled with the concept of destiny and life purpose. It's in all of us. As a pastor, I've counseled scores of sharp, educated and successful people who admitted behind closed doors that they desperately longed for a sense of purpose in life. Destiny is far more than a meaningful job. It has to do with who we are in discovering our unique niche in life. We all fear going to our graves without leaving our mark on society. Destiny is about the mark. The typical cemetery gravestone lists the deceased's year of birth and year of death. The numbers are separated by a dash. Destiny is about the substance of the dash.

A *pastor* has been defined as someone who talks in other people's sleep. As Terry says, it's been his experience that far too many people in life are sleepwalking. They're busy making a living—but they fail to make a life. What we're talking about goes back to what this book is all about, helping you discover why you were placed on Planet Earth. While there are no easy answers or magic formulas, there are practical principles to help you understand who you were meant to become. Savor the contents of this book, and awaken the sleeping giant within you. God has placed you here for a reason—now read this excellent work and fulfill it.

—Alan Nelson, Ed.D.

Author of *My Own Worst Enemy*
The Five Star Leader
Spiritual Intelligence

Introduction
Destined for
an Awakening

My life's work can easily be traced back to the moment when I was first awakened to the purpose of my being. From the time I was a child I knew exactly what I wanted to be in life. As all my childhood friends processed through the normal adolescent career choices—fireman, policeman, astronaut and doctor—I was fixated on two vocations: ministry and wildlife management. Family lore has it that when asked at three years of age, "What do you want to be when you grow up, little boy?", I enthusiastically replied, "A game warden and a preacher of the gospel!" Although I never pursued my love for the outdoors as a career choice, I have spent the past twenty years planting churches, training leaders and preaching the gospel on the soil of over sixty nations.

I realize that my story is somewhat unusual in that very few people approach life with the same degree of focus and intensity. Most of us discover our purpose through trial and error—the process of refining our gifts and talents and summoning the courage to act on what we believe in. The world is filled with the stories of remarkable individuals who refused to quit exploring their options and opportunities until they discovered their mission in life. Consider the salesman who experiences a series of painful failures only to finally awaken to his true gifting in some other field of business. Or the homemaker who lives with a deep-seated lack of fulfillment until she returns to college, finishes her education and devotes her life to teaching underprivileged children.

Some of the most effective ministries in history have been born out of a personal crisis. It may be a ministry to hurting women birthed through a painful divorce, a dynamic youth ministry developed by a young man who was raised in a broken home or an inner-city ministry started by a former member of a gang. Regardless of whether we discover our destiny at an early age in life, through the process of eliminating what doesn't work for us or by personal revelation, true purpose can only grasped by the "fully awakened." Most people fail to discover their destiny because they have never been spiritually illumined to the opportunity to be something more than what they are.

John Walsh, the televised crusader of justice, is a classic example of this principle. His personal awakening came on the heels of the kidnapping and murder of his six-year-old son, Adam. Resigning his partnership in a hotel management company, John dedicated his life to bringing criminals to justice and founded the nationally televised program *America's Most Wanted.* As of this writing, he has been instrumental in recovering over fifty-seven thousand missing children. CBS television recently named him as one of the "100 Americans Who Changed History."

In her novel *The Accidental Tourist*, Anne Tyler tells the story of a young couple whose son is murdered. This tragedy begins the process of unraveling their fragile marriage, little by little, until they are finally at the point of legal separation. In one poignant conversation, the wife turns to her husband in exasperation and says, "Nothing ever touches you anymore. You just drift through life." He is silent for a long moment, and then, really more to himself than to her, quietly murmurs, "I don't drift. I endure."[1]

Many people are drifting through life, desperately in need of a spiritual awakening. Awakenings unveil the purpose of our lives. Our awareness of our destiny often determines our reception of everything God has planned for us during the process of development. Therefore, an *awakening* is simply a moment of divine revelation in which new insight or new understanding is gained. An awakening will reveal what you have never seen before and position you for what you have never experienced. With this new understanding, the experiences of life are perceived differently, and new possibilities emerge. Once your eyes have been opened to see God's plan for your life, you will begin to experience transformation in your thoughts, emotions and behavior.

There comes a time in most of our lives when we grow tired of dead-end living and we see our need for an awakening. This is the moment, when in the midst of all your fears and uncertainty, you stop dead in your tracks, and you hear the voice of the Lord saying, *Enough is enough!* Enough dead-end living. Enough frustration and confusion. Enough barrenness and hopelessness. Enough pain and despair. And like a child quieting down after an outburst, your sobs begin to subside, you shudder once or twice, you blink back your tears and, through a veil of wet lashes, you begin to look at the world through new eyes.

This is your awakening.

To awaken is to discover the greatness of God. Just as your uniqueness is not the result of your personal ingenuity but rather the design of God, so your destiny is the end result of His magnificent plan for your life. The same Creator who takes painstaking care to insure that no two snowflakes are constructed the same, and that each fingerprint is remarkably distinct, also constructs your future with love and consideration.

To awaken is to begin building healthy and meaningful relationships. It is painful to face the fact that you are not perfect and that not everyone will always love, appreciate or approve of who or what you are. But that discovery is equally liberating. When you stop blaming other people for the things they did to you (or didn't do for you), you will realize the importance of accepting and appreciating who God created you to be. This is when you also learn that no one can do it all alone and that it's necessary to risk asking for help.

To awaken is to learn that principles such as responsibility and integrity are not the outdated ideals of a bygone era but the mortar that holds together the foundation upon which you must build a life. When these principles are clarified and accepted, it becomes much easier to set personal goals and boundaries and to focus on your own individual assignment. The only cross you are required to bear is the one you have been chosen by God to carry. Every flag is not yours to wave, and every hill is not yours on which to die.

To awaken is to learn that to succeed you need the power of a prophetic vision. When we lift our eyes to see the future destination for our lives, we are empowered to discover the daily pathway that leads us there. And as we step out in faith to pursue God's plan for our lives, we learn to step right through our fears, knowing that with God's grace we can handle whatever life throws at us.

To awaken is to realize that it's time to stop hoping and waiting for something to change or for happiness, safety and security to come galloping over the next horizon. Life is not a fairy tale. It's not a sitcom television program where every complex problem results in a happy ending within twenty-eight minutes and thirty seconds. The process of perfecting our purpose involves blood, sweat and tears—the commitment to become who we are created to be in spite of how long it takes to emerge and how painful it is to become. Yet even in the midst of the process we can be confident in knowing that "He who has begun a good work in you will complete it until the day of Jesus Christ."[2]

As you read this book, I pray that your heart would be awakened to these vital principles: the greatness of God; the power of healthy relationships; the importance of character; the ability to see beyond the immediate; the freedom to be who you are in Christ; and a commitment to persevere. These are the foundations of this elusive phenomenon called *destiny*.

—Terry M. Crist

Sleepless in Scottsdale

Section I

The Awakening

Awakened to Destiny

Profiles
in Destiny

Profiles in Destiny

A lonely orphan, he had plenty of time to concentrate on his one great love—baseball. While playing the outfield for the Marshalltown, Iowa, team, he was located by a professional scout from Chicago. Soon after, he was contracted to play for the beloved Chicago White Sox. His dreams were beginning to be realized. Dedicating his life to greater discipline, he excelled in outrunning all of his teammates, and in his first season he led the White Sox in stealing bases.

In one year alone, he stole ninety-five bases, setting a new world record. The country boy from Marshalltown seemed to be on his way to making a permanent place for himself in baseball glory.

But everything changed when he met and fell in love with a girl from the Jefferson Park Presbyterian Church. His love for her led to another deeper-held devotion, and it eclipsed his passion for baseball. He had finally discovered his personal destiny. His new career placed him before large crowds and, in one sense, he still performed to the cheers of the masses, but it was quite different from running down the baseline.

Though he lived in the days long before radio and television, he appeared before one hundred million people in his lifetime!

"Take a stand, and get into the game!" was one of his favorite slogans.

It is said that he introduced at least a million people into this new kind of life. But it was a different game with a different crowd, and it was for a different cause.

The man who never forgot baseball was the man who played his best game for God—America's greatest revival preacher: outfielder and base-stealer Billy Sunday.

Chapter 1

Confessions of a Recovering Sleepwalker

I have a confession to make.

I come from a long line of sleepwalkers. My ancestors were not your ordinary, run-of-the-mill, garden-variety class of sleepwalkers—they were the vanguard of the sleepwalking community. I am, in fact, convinced that my family perfected the art of sleepwalking, or at least elevated the status of sleepwalkers throughout the modern world.

Take, for instance, my Uncle Randy who crawled into the comfort of his soft bed one evening and awoke the following morning on the cold slats of the front porch swing. It seems my grandmother had opened his bedroom window shortly before he went to bed, and in the middle of the night, Randy, unaware of what he was doing, climbed out of bed, out the window and fell from the second story to the soft grass below. Still asleep, he stumbled over to the front porch where he curled up on the old-fashioned swing and continued his peaceful rest. My grandparents, who had spent the evening

1

entertaining a visiting minister, stopped by his bedroom to close the window and discovered he was missing. Realizing that he hadn't walked through the living room where they had been, they carefully searched the house and couldn't find him anywhere. Desperate, they finally called the police, and the search intensified. One officer happened to walk by the old porch swing where he found Randy, still sleeping.

Then, there is my father—a highly regimented man, degreed, disciplined, dedicated to his family and the ministry. But some people might call him "deranged" because of one peculiarity—he walks in his sleep.[1] As a matter of fact, he has been known to mumble, babble, preach sermons and even lecture my mother in his sleep. During one nightly episode he tore an old canvas feather pillow in half. On another occasion he even accused my sainted mother of looking like a gorilla. (To his defense, when I saw her in those curlers the next morning, she frightened me, too.)

His most bizarre sleepwalking episode took place when I was a child. In all fairness, he was under a lot of stress at the time. He was studying hard to complete his college degree while also caring for a young family when he found himself temporarily without a job due to a company strike. Much to his relief, he was finally called back to work. The night before his return he was extremely anxious. Worried that he would be late to work the next morning, he finally fell into a restless sleep. An hour or so later he awoke with a start, thinking he had missed the alarm clock—only to realize that very little time had passed and it was still the middle of the night. However, just to make sure that he was on time the next morning, he crawled out of bed, put his work pants on and climbed back into bed. Another hour passed, and he anxiously awoke again. This time he put on his shirt before climbing back into bed. This process repeated itself several times during the night with other articles of clothing until he was fully dressed, lying in bed in a restless state of sleep.

Now here's where it gets scary. Sometime just before dawn,

his subconscious mind took over. He crawled out of bed, picked up his car keys, opened the door to the house, walked down the sidewalk, climbed into the car and stuck the keys into the ignition—and woke up! Terror struck his heart as he realized just how close to danger he had been. From that time on my mother took extraordinary precautions to make sure that she knew his every movement in the middle of the night.

My neurosis is just as peculiar without being nearly as outrageous. Although I have never been much of a sleepwalker, my eccentricity involves sleep talking. On many occasions I have attempted to engage my wife in intense discussions regarding every imaginable topic while she tries convincing me that I am sound asleep and acting the fool. As strange as it sounds, medical research reveals that sleepwalkers are not aware of the fact that they are not awake. In fact, the exact opposite is true. Many sleepwalkers are convinced that they are fully lucid, especially if they are demonstrating a behavior seen in a dream or if they are expressing an action that has been programmed into their subconscious.

> **Dreams are true while they last; and do we not live in dreams?**
>
> —*Lord Tennyson*

Thankfully, none of the sleepwalkers in our family have been harmed in their nocturnal wanderings, and we have all developed a wonderful sense of humor in the process.

Blinded by the Night

Now, before you judge my family too harshly, let me share some medical facts about sleepwalking. Researchers have discovered that approximately 2 percent of the adults and 4 percent of the children in our nation are somnambulists—more commonly known as sleepwalkers—and my family fits right in the middle of the spectrum. One prominent researcher on sleepwalking discovered an entire family that got up every evening with remarkable regularity, found their way to the kitchen and sat around a large table where they eventually woke up. Researchers call this temporal sleepwalking, which means that a sleepwalker will arise every night at the same time and usually focus on the same objective—though rarely does it occur in an entire family.

Despite its name, however, sleepwalking is not actually the act of walking in your sleep. Most sleepwalkers are semiconscious, but oblivious to their condition, which is why they can negotiate around obstacles and perform simple acts. Although they often appear glassy-eyed and respond with slurred, single-word speech, they are subconsciously awake. William Shakespeare described the general state of all sleepwalkers when he said of Lady Macbeth: "You see, her eyes are open, but her sense is shut!"

Though few people ever experience the unusual family traits I described at the beginning of this chapter, the vast majority of people in our generation have been content to stumble through life with open eyes and closed senses. Like zombies in the 1968 cult film *Night of the Living Dead*, they lurch through the night with the preprogrammed movements of a robot, oblivious to the world of the living. These are the spiritual sleepwalkers in every generation who do not realize that there is a higher state of consciousness to be discovered and a greater quality of life to be lived. Believing that life offers nothing more than immediate gratification, they have settled for the world of slumber. They are asleep to this remarkable phenomenon freely offered to all mankind, this marvel called *destiny.*

Surrounded by Sleepwalkers

We are told in Genesis that "a deep sleep fell over Adam"— but nowhere in the Bible does it say that he woke up! It seems logical to assume that he did, because we see him acting in ways that seems congruent with people who are awake. But, in essence, Adam was the first spiritual sleepwalker.

Two classes of spiritual sleepwalkers can be found present in every generation. Both are unaware of their spiritual state.

The first are the individuals who have never been awakened to the plan of redemption for their lives and for the world. Blinded by "the god of this world," the eyes of their hearts have never been opened to see the purpose of their existence, their reason for being.

The second are the people who have experienced the initial awakening that occurs at conversion, but are still asleep to their own individual destinies in life. Their eyes have never been opened to "know what is the hope of His [Christ's] calling, what are the riches of the glory of His inheritance in the saints."[2]

> **Even where sleep is concerned, too much is a bad thing.**
>
> —*Homer*

Eyes never opened to redemption

There are at least four different words that describe metaphorically an individual who exists apart from Christ. Each references the same spiritual state of being. Before coming into a living relationship with the resurrected Christ, we were *dead, blind, lost* and *asleep*.[3] This is the first condition of fallen man—he has settled for a much lower human experience than he is entitled to through Jesus Christ.

Isn't it ironic that we were dead and yet alive at the same time? It's a paradox that many people cannot seem to grasp. We can be alive to the temporal, fleshly, carnal, sensual, earthly way of living, but dead to the purposes of God. Before we came to Christ, our bodies were alive to sin and our souls were alive to unrighteousness, but our spirits were asleep to the purpose of time and eternity. Prior to faith in Christ, we were spiritual sleepwalkers, externally alive yet internally asleep.

Man, in his natural condition, is dead to the purpose of God, which obviously leaves him spiritually blind to it. Adam's sin eradicated our vision; it put us to sleep and left us to stumble through life without any spiritual awareness of our divine destiny. The purpose of life for the unsaved man generally goes no further than the physical, temporal, material aspects of life. Eternity is not a matter that most unbelievers seem to spend much time even considering. They are devoid of understanding the spiritual issues of life.

The apostle Paul once described the unsaved as "having their understanding darkened, being alienated from the life of God, because of the ignorance that is in them, because of the blindness [hardness] of their heart."[4] The unsaved man does not have the spiritual faculties to comprehend life in the kingdom. He cannot even see the road to redemption.

A lost person (one who does not know Christ as Savior and Lord) is blind, which is precisely why he is lost. He is not necessarily lost because he chooses to be. He is lost because he has not yet been found. Sometimes we Christians forget what it was like to be lost. Judgmentally, we say of others, "If they really wanted to be found they would be." But that's not necessarily true. Many are lost simply because they can't find their way home. They have little understanding of the deeper meaning of life, the need to prepare for eternity or the opportunity to participate in destiny. A blind person has no internal illumination to see the way, the truth and the life.

This is where the irresistible grace of God comes into play. Although we were lost, blind and asleep, God wasn't. When we couldn't find Him, He found us! When we didn't have the presence of mind to choose Him, He chose us! And when we gave up all our arguments and surrendered our lives to the lordship of Jesus Christ, the Holy Spirit came into our hearts and gave us brand-new spiritual faculties. He gave us eyes to see, ears to hear and hearts that are spiritually perceptive.

Asleep to God's purpose and destiny

The second category of sleepwalker involves those who are born again but still spiritually asleep to the purpose of God for their lives. They have responded to the opportunity to prepare for eternity, but they have not been illumined to the need to embrace destiny. This type of sleepwalker cannot distinguish between veracity and fantasy. Life, for them, is a series on shadows and illusions, all avoiding the harsh reality of the light of day.

We are asleep with compasses in our hands.

—Poet W. S. Merwin

In Mark 8, when Jesus arrived in Bethsaida a blind man was brought to Him for healing. In response to the faith of the crowd, Jesus did something very peculiar—He spit on the man before touching him. I can imagine the shock waves that must have gone through the crowd as Jesus offended their religious sensibilities. But the most surprising event was yet to come. Although the blind man improved, the healing was not complete. He needed another touch to clarify his blurred vision.[5]

The crowd must have been somewhat dismayed as the miracle momentarily hung somewhere between failure and success. When had it ever taken Jesus a *second* touch to heal anyone? Why now? Why this man? Was there a lesson to be learned here? Finally Jesus touched him again, and the miracle was complete. The first touch restored the man's vision, but a second touch was needed to restore his perception.

This first-century miracle exposes our deepest need with remarkable exactness. It symbolizes the journey that we are all on—the journey from darkness to light, from spiritual blindness to revelation. Like the blind man, when we come to Christ we experience the initial "opening of our eyes" through the experience of the new birth. For the first time in life we begin to "see" as we had never seen before.

The new-birth experience awakens us out of slumber. Yet we find ourselves living in the land of blurry vision, still struggling with the same dilemma that every other newborn Christian experiences. Because of the first touch of the Master Healer, we now have *vision*, but no *comprehension*. We have *eyesight*, but no *insight*. Our eyes have been opened to *see*, but not to *perceive*. We need another touch from God to awaken our spiritual senses. We need another spiritual awakening to move us beyond our first encounter with the grace of God so that we may comprehend the purpose for which we were born.

With keen insight Eugene Peterson mines this same principle from the treasure house of Philippians 3:15:

> So let's keep focused on that goal, those of us who want everything God has for us. If any of you have something else in mind, something less than total commitment, God will clear your blurred vision—you'll see it yet![6]

Spiritual Lethargica

Imagine falling to sleep one night only to wake up forty years later. As unlikely as it may seem, that premise serves as the basis for the critically acclaimed movie *Awakenings*, starring Robin Williams. This bizarre story could have been taken from the fairy tale of Rip Van Winkle, and yet it is true. The movie was loosely based on the true account of a young neurologist, Dr. Oliver Sacks, and his quest to solve a rare neurological disorder.

Immediately following World War I, an illness called *encephalitis lethargica* swept across Europe and America leaving millions of victims in its wake. The main symptom of this sleeping sickness was a comatose state that could last for months or even years. A few patients had even been comatose for decades. If the patients did eventually wake up (the majority died during the acute phase), they were likely to find themselves in the distorted condition of extreme Parkinson's patients, with rigidly twisted limbs, little or no mobility and a strangely suspended relationship to time. Most were in a vegetative condition with glassy eyes, blank stares and absolutely no response to doctors, nurses or loved ones.

Between 1916 and 1926, tens of thousands of disabled survivors, many of them vital young people who had been struck down in their late teens and early twenties, were eventually warehoused in chronic-care facilities and treated as the living dead. No one knew what to do with them. There was no proper treatment or cure. The nurses who fed them and cared for them would often insist that behind those frozen masks were fully intelligent personalities.

In 1966, a young neurologist, Dr. Oliver Sacks, was working at Beth Abraham Hospital in the Bronx in New York City. These post-encephalitic patients, frozen in their odd postures and parked in wheelchairs around the hospital, captured his attention. Dr. Sacks believed the nurses who said that there were vital sensibilities alive inside those statues. He gathered the sleeping-sickness victims (many of whom had been virtually ignored for forty years) into a community within the larger hospital. Eventually, after much internal and some external debate, he began to give them a new wonder drug, L-Dopa, which had proved remarkably effective in treating patients with Parkinson's disease. As Dr. Sacks increased the levels of medication in the patients, he was able to bring first one, and then others, back to a conscious awareness of life. It was an astonishing development that rocked the scientific community.

In the end the experiment failed. These patients were only able to awaken for brief periods before experiencing the devastating side effects of the medication. Dr. Sacks was finally forced to abandon the project and concede defeat, but not before seeing the wonder of their emergence out of this comatose condition into the modern world.[7]

Dr. Oliver Sacks's encounter with this rare disorder is analogous to the experience of every Christian. These survivors of encephalitis lethargica were alive in the sense that their bodies continued to function in a limited and distorted fashion, yet they were *asleep* to everything that gives meaning and purpose to life. To prevent spiritual lethargica from impacting the believers at Colosse, Paul reminded them of all that God had placed within them because of their relationship to Christ. He challenged them to awaken to the reality of their identity in Christ.[8]

We were all victims of *spiritual lethargica*—spiritual sleeping sickness—before we were awakened to life in Christ. The curse of sin left us in a twisted, distorted condition. We were unaware—frozen and comatose—to the meaning and purpose of life. We had no understanding of why we were created in the image of God. Only by the grace of God, administered through the new-birth experience, were we brought from that comatose, vegetative state called *sin* into a glorious awakening in Christ. Our awakening to life in Christ also empowered us to begin the process of awakening to the destiny God has chosen for us.

Sleeping on a Bus Called Destiny

Shortly after Judith and I were married, we went on a study tour of the Middle East. Exhausted from the pressures of balancing a new marriage along with significant ministry responsibilities, I found it impossible to stay awake and focused throughout the trip. The droning sound from the engine of the tour bus put me to sleep. The monotone voice of the tour guide put me to sleep. The warm sun on my face put me to sleep. Even the rhythmic motion of riding the donkey down into Petra put me to sleep! When everyone else in the tour disembarked from the bus to see another point of interest, I remained behind snoozing. Try as I did, I simply could not remain awake. I was snoring my way across the Holy Land.

During the nineteen years since that disappointing trip, "sleeping on the bus" has come to be a metaphor my wife has gently used on many occasions to describe my inattentiveness to important issues. As much as I would like to say otherwise, there have been times when I have slept through significant moments in our life together—a forgotten birthday, a misinterpreted expression, a missed opportunity never to be recovered.

I've since discovered that I'm not alone in my propensity toward spiritual narcolepsy. Many well-meaning Christians are sleeping on a bus called *Destiny*, snoring their way through the greatest moments of their lives. Their inattentiveness has come to characterize the pattern of a life going nowhere. To paraphrase the words of the apostle Paul, "It is high time to awake out of sleep" lest you find yourself alone, sleeping on the bus, in the middle of the desert.[9]

By the way, the cost of the tour is the same whether you learn anything or not!

The best way to make your dreams come true is to wake up.

—*J. M. Powers*

Profile of a Sleepwalker

Joe was a young sleepwalker who first visited our church in the late 1980s. A talented athlete, he was drafted by the Chicago Cubs and spent the years following high school playing baseball in Europe before accepting a scholarship to play for Oral Roberts University. As a committed Christian with strong denominational roots, Joe had a firm grasp on eternity but not destiny. He had the foresight to prepare for death but lacked the insight to prepare for life. Little did he know that an ordinary Sunday morning was going to change his life...forever.

He later described his experience as an "awakening" as he saw purpose reflected in the eyes of everyone around him—from the one who greeted him at the front door to the individual sitting next to him. As he witnessed the passionate display of worship, fervent prayer and powerful teaching, he began to sense that something vital was missing in his life. One visit turned into another, and before long a year went by. Each week contained a new discovery as Joe began to realize that as noble and worthy a vocation as professional baseball was, it could not even compare with his new passion—his true passion—to preach the gospel to others.

A decade has passed since that fateful encounter with the Holy Spirit, a praying community and a prophetic call to destiny. Joe now pastors a thriving church located in a small town in Western Kansas. We recently traveled together through many of the same European cities where he played baseball, this time training leaders to discover their purpose in life.

In sharing Joe's story, I run the risk of leading you to believe that the only place of true fulfillment in life is in full-time ministry. Nothing could be further from the truth. Throughout this book I will share the stories of many others who, like Joe, discovered that personal fulfillment is directly connected to the discovery of your individual destiny. Destiny is not a one-size-fits-all solution. It is as diverse and distinctive as we are as human beings.

Like Billy Sunday, the great baseball player turned preacher, Joe had spent the first phase of his life asleep to his higher purpose. And yet, unlike many other sleepwalkers, he had chosen to settle for what many aspiring athletes would consider the pinnacle of achievement. (Most people would not consider a career in baseball as a bad place to settle!) Many sleepwalkers are convinced that everyone else is living life at the same level they are, and they believe there is no higher reality than the world of slumber. Their mantra is, "Enjoy what you have because this is all life has to offer."

Spiritual sleepwalkers are incapable of responding to opportunity or to possibility. They subconsciously perform according to what circumstances dictate, generational curses determine or authority figures demand.

Spiritual sleepwalkers stumble blindly through the greatest

moments of development and fulfillment that life has to offer. They falter through the most important developmental stages of life—home, church, school and college—before settling for a mediocre career, an unfulfilling marriage and perhaps even a nominal religious experience. But God has much greater designs on our lives than to settle for spiritual sleepwalking. He offers us the possibility of living life with our vision clear and our hearts filled with passion, purpose and productivity.

Your Point of View Matters

There are two views of life: the earthly perspective and the heavenly perspective. We live in the midst of a generation that looks at everything from the natural, earthly point of view. And I am not just talking about unbelievers—I am talking about humanistic Christians. It is possible for people to give their lives to Christ but never renew their minds. Therefore, rather than thinking *theistically* (thinking the biblical way about life), they are resigned to thinking *humanly*—looking at things from a carnal, fleshly, temporal earthly point of view.

Several years ago, as I was reading in the Book of Revelation, one phrase leaped out at me: "Those who dwell on the earth."[10] Earth dwellers live life from a natural materialistic point of view and never think about looking up. Philippians 3 says they "set their mind on earthly things."[11] These "earth dwellers" keep their nose in the dust and never look up to the greatness, the beauty, the power and the triumph of their salvation. It never dawns on them that there is a higher way of living.

Let me illustrate it this way: Picture a farmer in the hog pen at feeding time. He gets a few ears of corn and calls the hogs, and they run to the fence. The farmer drops a few kernels of corn on the ground, and the hogs eat them and keep rooting around in the dirt for more. All the while the farmer has the rest of the corn in his hands up above them. The hogs just continue rooting in the ground. It never occurs to them that the corn is up above.

Many people never look up. It never dawns on them that "every good gift and every perfect gift is from above, and comes down from the Father of lights, with whom there is no variation or shadow of turning."[12] Their earthly point of view taints every beautiful gift from God with hopelessness and despair.

But the beauty of our redemption is that you do not have to spend your life looking at things from an earthly point of view. Your position in Christ opens your eyes to a new perspective—a new you means a new view. The Father has "raised us up together, and made us sit together in the heavenly places in Christ Jesus."[13] If you have ever been on a mountaintop and looked out over a valley with a winding stream running through it, you can see where the stream is going. But when you are down in the valley standing beside the stream—then you only see the area of the stream that's right in front of you.

Have you ever wondered why some people consistently miss opportunities to advance in their relationships, careers and spiritual development? How can they settle for going through the motions rather then maximizing the moments? Why have they lost the ability to respond properly to the environment in which they find themselves—or did they ever have it to begin with? It can be extremely frustrating to witness the untapped potential lying dormant in the lives of those we love when we know they are capable of living at a higher level. But the greatest frustration comes in knowing that they cannot even see their own potential.

Perhaps you find yourself in the same predicament when it comes to your own personal destiny. You see where you have been with far greater clarity than where you are going. Your greatest problem is not in a lack of *foresight*—it is in a lack of *insight*. Many times our foresight is virtually nonexistent, even though our hindsight is 20/20, simply because insight is the key to the mysterious doorway called the future. As renowned economist and futurist Gary Hamel once said, "Perspective is worth fifty IQ points."[14] Spiritual insight is a vital necessity in order to find and fulfill your purpose in life.

Henry David Thoreau, naturalist, philosopher and author of *Walden*, once remarked, "The mass of men lead lives of quiet desperation."[15] Despair is the consequence of purposelessness. Purposelessness is the result of spiritual blindness. When we fail to see the opportunities that God has provided for us to become everything He has destined us to be, we resign to lead lives of quiet desperation. To be awakened is to be empowered to act.

> **What lies behind us and what lies before us are little matters compared to what lies within us.**
>
> —*Oliver Wendell Holmes*

In my work as a spiritual coach and mentor, I consistently interact with brilliant men and women who have analyzed the present, contemplated the future and mapped out a reasonable plan of action, yet they still fail to fulfill the purpose for which they were born. They are frustrated because intellect—and not illumination—is driving their purpose in life. But intelligent foresight is not enough to insure that you will reach the destination that God has chosen for you. Perhaps that's why Paul prayed that the eyes of our understanding would be enlightened. It takes revelation, insight and illumination to produce the spiritual passion that will empower you to reach your God-chosen destination. That's why we need an encounter with the God who awakens men.

Seeing Into Your Destiny

1. Can you identify the areas of your life that are spiritually asleep? What are they?

2. Are you fulfilled in your marriage, career, ministry and relationships? In what ways do you long for something more?

3. Have you clarified your hopes and dreams for the future? Can you define them?

4. Can you choose your own awakening, or is it beyond your control?

5. What action can you take to encourage your own awakening as you read this book? Prayer? Fasting? Worship?

Profiles
in Destiny

Profiles in Destiny

Born the son of a Baptist minister in the Deep South during the 1920s, Martin Luther King Jr. was no stranger to segregation. Throughout his childhood he was constantly reminded of the fact that prejudice ran rampant and that there was no sign of its subsidence. His childhood was marred by periodic bouts of depression, which led to two failed suicide attempts.

In spite of his battle with depression, he sailed through school with little effort, periodically skipping grades, and entered Morehouse College at the age of fifteen. His plans were to become a doctor or a lawyer, but the college president influenced him to consider the ministry. He graduated from Crozer Theological Seminary in 1951 and eventually received a Ph.D. in systematic theology from Boston College. His life took an uncertain turn when a young black seamstress refused to give up her seat on the bus.

On that day in 1955, Rosa Parks refused to give up her bus seat to a white man and was jailed on the pretext of having violated segregation laws. This event was the spark that ignited the Civil Rights movement, which was spearheaded by Dr. King. He protested the wrongful segregation and discrimination of minorities in America, and on more than one occasion he risked his life knowingly for his cause.

Dr. Martin Luther King Jr. had a dream. It was for the complete equality and harmony between blacks and whites, and it was that for which he ultimately gave his life in 1968. The result of his dream is that segregation has been eradicated in our nation, and discrimination has diminished considerably. But one question still remains: Had Rosa Parks not stood up for her rights by resisting the unjust laws of Alabama, would Dr. King's dream have ever become a reality?

Chapter 2
The God Who Awakens Men

There's a divinity that shapes our ends. Roughhew them how we will.

—William Shakespeare

Sovereignty. The word conjures up mysterious images of a God we cannot ever hope to understand. Infinitely wise and inescapably mystical, He veils Himself in shrouded images, puzzling codes, spiritual types and dark shadows. For most Christians, trying to define the "sovereignty of God" is like trying to decipher the grainy images flitting across a television screen on a stormy night. Having been taught that this sovereign God cannot be identified with any reasonable assurance, they remain in confusion and turmoil—never knowing quite what to expect from this One who changes His character in much the same way a chameleon changes colors.

But that is not the God of the Bible.

The God who awakens men delights in self-disclosure. He desires to reveal Himself to our finite understanding. He rejoices in our comprehension of His character. But the disclosure of His personhood and His eternal purpose for our lives is always on *His terms*, not ours. He reserves the revelation of divine destiny for those who diligently seek Him. Why? Because the search refines our motives, attitudes and ambitions.

The God who delights in our discovery of His person requires that the search be conducted on His terms. That's why He invites us to search for Him with our whole hearts.[1]

I can remember as though it were yesterday when my children were toddlers learning to play hide-and-seek. At first they believed that if they covered their face their entire bodies were covered. As they grew older and the game progressed, they learned that the real joy was not in hiding but in being discovered. With the stealth of a lumbering elephant and the snorts of an enraged bull I would charge through the house chanting, "Fee, fie, fo, fum. I smell the blood of a Crist young'un." Finally their nerve would break, and they would snicker, squeal, squirm and disclose their hiding place. Their "capture" was followed by peals of laughter as my fingers insistently tickled their ribs. The joy was in the discovery.

And then it would be my turn to hide. Trying to disappear behind a dining room chair is not an easy task for a grown man, but I welcomed the challenge. The confused counting of an excited child usually went "1, 2, 5, 9, 10"—and the chase was on with another round of, "Fee, foe, fum, fie, I smell the buud of a Crist dadee." (I never claimed my children were poetic.) Before long we were back in a loving pile of hugs, kisses and peals of laughter.

As I write the above paragraph, the memory brings a smile to my face.

So it is with the God who awakens men. The sovereign God, who may even appear to be hiding from us, longs to be discovered. He desires to awaken to destiny those who long to be awakened. The clues are freely given to believers and nonbelievers alike. He gives us hints of His deity through our inner longings and the beauty of creation. Every mountain that begs to be climbed and every ocean that entices men to cross it is the evidence of the God who delights in self-disclosure. The natural world is a clue to the delight we will experience when we lay aside our selfish ways of living so that we can search for Him with all our heart.

Sleeping by a Fire Called Destiny

The God who awakens men reserves the revelation of His will and His ways to those who seek Him on His terms. The search requires commitment, diligence and holy passion.[2] If the discovery and development of your destiny is of little value to you, don't expect Him to seek you out and demand that you "come participate with Me in the eternal purpose I have chosen for you." The disciples learned this the hard way.

Matthew 26 records the apathetic attitude of these potential world shakers who were not only physically slumbering, but also were spiritually asleep to the purposes of the kingdom. While Jesus was in the Garden of Gethsemane, struggling with the painful process that positioned Him for His ultimate destiny and for the redemption of the planet, His disciples were fast asleep around a campfire called *Destiny*. Three times He came back from the inner court of the Garden to the outer field where they slept to ask them, "Can't you stick it out with me a single hour? Stay alert; be in prayer..."[3]

> **The sovereign being is burdened with a servitude that crushes him, and the condition of free men is servility.**
>
> —*George Bataille*

We will never know what kind of impact that lost hour of prayer with Jesus could have made in the lives of the disciples. It was a lost opportunity. I've often wondered how many golden opportunities we lose because we are *spiritually asleep* to the gentle voice of Christ imploring us to "stick it out with Him."

I have often wondered if the disciples failed to stay awake

because of their lack of spiritual insight into the purpose of the Garden experience. Many times our failure to persevere is the result of not having seen the purpose of the moment. As a P. K. (preacher's kid) I spent the first few years of my life drooling under the front pew of the church because I had little insight into the real purpose for our church services. When I discovered the purpose of the corporate gathering, I quit sleeping under the pew. I had been awakened to a higher objective.

Awakening to Majesty

Many people spend their lives sleeping under the pew because they fail to understand God's sovereignty and how it relates to our need to make personal choices in life.

Failing to understand God's sovereignty and how it relates to our need to make personal choices can lead to frustration and, in some cases, even to self-destruction. Because our beliefs determine our behavior, our view of God's sovereignty determines the degree of responsibility we assume in fulfilling our destiny.

God's sovereignty affects far more than our election (salvation); it touches all of life. It has immense bearing on the way we live, regardless of whether we understand the finer points of the doctrine. As Greek scholar Arthur Pink observes, the doctrine of sovereignty is "the foundation of Christian theology… the center of gravity in the system of Christian truth—the sun around which all lesser orbs are grouped."[4] Thus, to welcome and embrace the right of the sovereign Lord to rule our lives is to live at peace with the provision and plans He has made for us.

God's right to govern our lives is based upon the fact that He is the sovereign Creator, Ruler and Sustainer of all things. The word *sovereign* is both a noun and a verb. As a verb it means "to rule," and as a noun it means "king," "master" or "supreme ruler." Therefore, God is above all in authority and power, and He possesses the incontestable right to govern all things according to the counsel of His own will.[5] To acknowledge the sovereignty of God is to recognize that He has absolute power, authority and autonomy and is ultimately in charge of the entire universe, from eternity past to eternity future.

I love the fourth chapter of Acts. The church was in its infancy, and the world had become a nursery for born-again believers. As they reached out to change the world, the backlash was intense. Many of the new Christians were beaten, others were imprisoned, and still others, murdered. When they gathered to pray, they identified almighty God by a noteworthy title. "When they heard this, they raised their voices together in prayer to God. 'Sovereign Lord,' they said, 'you made the heaven and the earth and the sea, and everything in them.'"[6] You can learn a lot about an individual's perception of God by what they call Him. Their recognition of Him as sovereign Lord means they understood that you can never get beyond the grasp of His ability to intervene in our lives and in our circumstances.

The *Westminster Confession of Faith* also acknowledges the sovereign authority of God when it declares:

> God, from eternity, did, by the most wise and holy counsel of His own will, freely, and unchangeably ordain whatever comes to pass.[7]

Nothing catches God by surprise. All things that He foreordained from eternity past are destined to work out in the generation for which He reserves them. When we consider the importance of fulfilling our destinies, we should think in terms of serving our generation according to God's purposes. That service could be serving Habitat for Humanity or discovering a cure for cancer. It could be pastoring a small rural church or training future leaders in the classrooms of an Ivy League university. Whatever our destiny, no words could be a better epitaph than those accorded King David at his death: "For David, after he had served his own generation by the will of God, fell asleep, was buried with his fathers..."[8]

What enabled David to serve the purpose of God unlike any other king in Israel? Could it be his understanding of the importance of cooperating with the sovereign God's choice for his life? It was David who first discovered, "All the days ordained for me were written in your book before one of them came to be."[9]

What exactly does that mean? Is God a cosmic puppeteer, pulling the strings of human marionettes? Does He sovereignly determine what we are destined for without considering our personal preferences? Or do we have a degree of personal sovereignty with the right either to invite Him into our affairs or to restrict His personal involvement? Are our lives a product of God's sovereignty or of human responsibility? Or are they the result of both, each fulfilling a unique part of His eternal purpose? And, perhaps most importantly, if God is in complete control of everything, including human choice, then how can we be truly free? Christians have wrestled with these very questions for centuries.

Sovereign Over Man

One of the most difficult areas for most people to grasp is God's sovereignty over man. Most of us have little difficulty acknowledging God's sovereignty over the rest of Creation—after all, nature does not have a will of its own. If God chooses to exercise His sovereign authority over weather systems and earthquakes, over plants, animals, trees, rivers, mountains and valleys—what is that to us? But to believe that God ultimately governs the actions of man seems to invalidate the free will of man and makes him no more than a puppet on a woodcarver's bench.

The Almighty has His own purposes.

—*Abraham Lincoln*

Yet the Bible repeatedly affirms God's governorship over humanity. One of the clearest examples of God's unlimited scope of authority is found in God's rulership over Pharaoh. Even this cruel, depraved, despot was but a fleshly pawn in the hands of the Sovereign One.[10]

Another scripture dealing with the subservience of humanity is found in Proverbs 21: "The king's heart is in the hand of the LORD, like the rivers of water; He turns it wherever He wishes."[11] Have you ever attempted to change the course of a river? It is impossible to do so and fully benefit from the natural course God intended for it to take.

Before the construction of the Aswan High Dam, the Nile River rolled through a series of six rapids, called *cataracts*, between Northern Sudan and Southern Egypt. Since the completion of the dam, the river has gradually changed its course. In one generation, life as it existed for thousands of years along the Nile River has been irrevocably altered. The once rich soil is now depleted, the wildlife forced into other habitats and the temperature altered because of the diminishing depth of the river and the increasing size of the lake. These are the effects of changing the course of just one river. Yet God directs the course of billions of lives, none more important than the life of the king.

Accomplished scholar Charles Bridges comments insightfully on this verse in Proverbs 21:

> The general truth [of God's sovereignty over the hearts of people] is taught by the strongest illustration—His uncontrollable sway upon the most absolute of all wills—the king's heart.[12]

It is difficult today for those of us in Western cultures who have been indoctrinated in the value of living in a democratic republic to fully understand the dynamics of living under the rule of an unlimited monarchy. Most contemporary monarchies are restricted, and the royal families rule symbolically rather than literally. But in Solomon's day, the king was an absolute monarch. He ruled without restraint. No legislature could veto his laws, and no supreme court could control his actions. The king's word was final. His authority was absolute. Yet, the king's heart was in the hand of the Lord. God gave us this illustration to show that all hearts are under His divine control. Even the man who refuses to answer to anyone still answers to God.

The most stubborn will is but water in the hand of the Lord. He governs the affairs of those who invite Him and those who resist Him—although the latter do not fully benefit from the opportunity to partner with God in the fulfillment of their destiny. All of us move in response—either in concert with or frustration against—His sovereign influence. None can resist His supreme authority. He governs men, nations and history with the same resolve. And if God still governs the most resistant of hearts, then surely He has our lives firmly under His control— whether we are celebrated or tolerated, received or rejected, honored or dishonored, abounded or abased.

Who Has the Final Word?

At times it may seem as if our destinies are in the hands of other people. Their decisions seem to determine our successes or failures. An employer can promote or demote our career. A teacher can advance or restrain our education. A parent can equip or restrict our life skills. While we may work to the best of our ability to counteract the negative influences that prevent us from fulfilling our divine destinies, we often feel powerless to change the forces of life that seem to be against us. Yet even in those times—especially in those times—God is still sovereignly in control of our lives. His sovereign authority cannot be restrained or resisted where our futures are concerned.

> **Whatever God has brought about is to be borne with courage.**
>
> —*Sophocles*

Perhaps no life illustrates the sovereignty of God more than that of Joseph.[13] Raised in an unhealthy family culture, betrayed by his brothers, sold into slavery, framed by the wife of his master and thrown into prison—it looked as if everything had come to a screeching halt for Joseph. But it didn't, because Joseph's life wasn't in the hands of his brothers, the master who purchased him or the keeper of the prison. Joseph's life was firmly under the sovereign authority of almighty God, who says, "I will work and no one will restrain me."[14] In due time, God's purpose for Joseph was established—and that purpose saved a nation from starvation and preserved the family of Jacob (Israel), whose twelve sons became the twelve tribes of Israel.

The Benefits of Understanding God's Sovereignty

It awakens the soul to the virtue of meekness.

God's sovereignty is a very humbling doctrine. It reminds us that God is God, and we are not. When we think we're ready to advise God on how to run the universe, He just looks at us and says, "How many stripes do you have on your sleeve?" It's like a person who visits my house and starts to criticize things. Perhaps he doesn't like the shade of marble tile in the foyer or our choice of artwork in the formal living room or even the flower arrangements on the dining room table. When he is finished with his criticism, only one comment is appropriate: "Whose name is on the title deed to this house? When you start paying the bills around here, you get a vote on the decorating. Until then, feel free to say nothing."

When I was growing up, my father often put it this way: "Son, as long as you eat my beans and taters and put your feet under my table, I'm in charge around here." That always signaled to me that the conversation was over. Absolutely over. The only way to avoid having "the board of education placed on my backside for the purpose of applied learning" was to say, "Yes, sir!" Sovereignty puts us in the place where we feel free to say nothing about the way God runs the universe.

The apostle James presents a practical and simple view of God's sovereignty, a view, I might add, that is often overlooked by many of us who become accustomed to governing our own lives without consulting God on the matter. He states, "Come now, you who say, 'Today or tomorrow we will go to such and such a city, spend a year there, buy and sell, and make a profit'; whereas you do not know what will happen tomorrow. For what is your life? It is even a vapor that appears for a little time and then vanishes away. Instead you ought to say, 'If the Lord wills, we shall live and do this or that.' But now you boast in your arrogance. All such boasting is evil."[15]

James is addressing people who tend to make ordinary business plans. In our contemporary setting this might be those who determine to build a business, plant a church, attend a university, buy a car or a home or choose a spouse. James does not condemn the action of planning. He doesn't even criticize the desire to make money. What he condemns is presumptuous planning—that is, plans that ignore the purposes of God and do not acknowledge the sovereignty of God to interrupt and change our plans. James simply says, "Whatever you do, let the Lord determine the course of it."

When I was a child growing up in a pastor's home, the old saints would always conclude a statement about the future with the phrase, "the Lord willing." While that phrase undoubtedly became a meaningless cliché for many people, it was intended to express awareness that our future is ultimately determined by the purpose of the sovereign Lord.

Yet most of us make plans without acknowledging that God is sovereign in all affairs and in every circumstance. We arrogantly say:

> Lord, I expect You to bless these plans I have made for my life. I am going to build this business, and I want Your favor. I am going to marry this individual, and I want Your blessing. I have chosen to live in this city, and I want your approval. Lord, here are my goals for my life. Read them and bless them!

And then we wonder why we continually live in frustration,

hitting our head against the wall of life, bumping up against the ceiling of God's plan for our life, frustrated because things don't seem to be going the way that we want them to go.

In our success-oriented culture, we have discovered the importance of developing a vision, writing a mission statement and constructing plans for the future. But there is a more fundamental place to begin the process of setting the course of our lives. *Ground zero* is where we tune our ears to heaven, humble ourselves in the presence of God and seek His will above all else. The individuals who prevail in a generation are those who discover God's perfect plan for their lives.[16] And those who frustrate their lives are those trying to do their own thing.

If the plan in our heart is the reflection of the Lord's purpose, then we have the formula for absolute victory. But if the desire of our heart is contrary to the purpose of God, we have the recipe for frustration and, in some extreme cases, even destruction. The key to fulfilling our dreams is to make sure they come from heaven. As the Lord's will triumphs, the purposes of a man's heart are accomplished.

Understanding the sovereignty of God produces genuine humility. I recognize that my life is but a vapor. I acknowledge that God is in charge and that His purpose will ultimately prevail. If I am going to live life in peace and in joy, I must discover the purpose of the Lord and work in conjunction with that.

It awakens the soul to the government of God.

One of the greatest problems in our generation is the diminishment of our perspective of God—we have lost the biblical perspective of His majestic greatness. As J. B. Phillips points out in his deeply stirring book *Your God Is Too Small*, most people today see God as the resident policeman, the grand old man, a parental hangover or some other short-sighted, twisted view of God.[17] Perhaps the greatest problem in Western Christianity is that our God is too small—He has somehow diminished over time. We read of His greatness in Genesis, His majesty in Exodus and His miraculous power in the Acts of the Apostles, but we fail to see Him the "same yesterday, today, and forever."[18]

To understand the sovereignty of God is to acknowledge that nothing began with us—and it probably won't end with us. We are only one part of God's unbroken stream from the foundation of the world. And if Jesus tarries for another fifty or hundred years, perhaps someone will write a paragraph about our generation in some future history book and keep moving forward into the opportunities on the horizon. We are simply a part of the successive, progressive work of God, and by His greatness we occupy a moment of time in a generation. We live in Him. We move in Him. We breathe in Him. And we do His will as long as He gives us life.

When our mission is complete and our time is over, He raises up another generation and continues to do what He has been doing from the foundation of the world. Nothing stops God in His eternal purpose. Nations rise...and fall...and are reborn under the banner of a new hope and a better government. Because of their love for one another, two individuals are married...children are born...raised...and released to form new families. Soon the two who originally formed the family pass from the scene. A church is born...it grows...is celebrated...and then dies a terrible death because of a split or moral failure in the leadership. Its death breaks all our hearts, but it doesn't stop the progressive work of the kingdom of God. The eternal purpose of God is greater than a nation, a family, a church or a generation.

Sometimes it is hard to see the greatness of God because our image blocks the Son. The key to seeing the greatness of God is not in making God larger, but in making ourselves smaller in our own eyes.

It awakens the soul to trust in God's faithfulness.

Perhaps one reason so many Christians are unhappy in our day is because we have lost the peace that comes only in trusting God to care for our lives. We can get so wrapped up in ourselves that we forget who God is, what He's capable of doing, what He's done in the past and the way He is currently moving on our behalf.

It is reported that the California Highway Department recently began tests on a potential freeway that incorporates a system of computerized cars and specialized magnetic message devices that have been installed in the roadway. The theory is that the computers and message devices would drive the car. All you have to do is program the destination, then sit back and relax as the computer drives the car at speeds of seventy-five miles per hour or more. There is only one problem—no one wants to ride in the cars.

Automotive engineers have the system in place on a test area and claim that the technology is working well, but they cannot get anyone to ride in the special cars at high speeds.[19] People are willing to get in and kind of putt-putt along, but when they turn the juice up, everybody wants out. Nobody trusts the system to work at high speeds. The problem is one of trust.

We have the same problem with God. We say, "If I am willing to open myself up to God's leadership in my life, if I am willing to submit my plans, decisions, my goals, my life to Him, then can I really trust Him? Can I count on a loving God to direct my life? Will He make the choices that lead to fulfillment and contentment, or will His choices for my life leave me empty and unsatisfied? Can I trust Him when things are moving full speed ahead or just when life is putt-putting along?"

Most people struggle with submitting to the sovereignty of God because of a lack of trust in Him. Knowing this, God goes on record permanently by saying that we can trust Him.[20]

If the God who created us...hard-wired us...the God who understands our needs even better than we understand them ourselves...if that God is unable to bring contentment and peace into our lives, then quite frankly, contentment and peace cannot be found in the universe. The corollary is simply that the One who created us—the manufacturer, the designer—knows us best.

Any parent can remember how frustrating it was trying to

interpret the cry of a newborn baby. With our three sons, there were times when Judith and I would say to one another, "If they could only talk!" But it can also be difficult to interpret the cries and needs of an adult.

As adults, we still have cries that we cannot interpret ourselves, cries that cannot be interpreted by spouses, pastors or friends—longings deep within our hearts that we are unable to express in words. We just know there is an emptiness that needs to be filled. When we cannot articulate our need we become angry, frustrated and miserable.

But there is One who can interpret the cries of His children, whether they are infants or adults. He is the One who designed us. Even when you can't articulate the longing in your heart, He understands. God hears the cry of the righteous. Even when you cannot form the words, God hears your heart when you cry in the night season. And He can be trusted. The One who created you knows best how to meet your longings and your desires. That is why you can be complete only in your relationship with Jesus Christ—and complete in no other.

The word which God has written on the brow of every man is hope.

—*Victor Hugo in* Les Míserables

We were created to be complete in Jesus Christ alone. St. Augustine described "a God-shaped hole" in our hearts that can be filled only by a vital relationship with the living God. Every generation since Adam has searched for something to fill the emptiness that arises from our separation from heaven. In his top hit "I Am I Said," Neil Diamond, one of the most successful singer/songwriters of several decades, wrote about the emptiness deep inside that would not let him go. That cry of his soul echoes in our own hearts when we hear him sing those words.

Viktor Frankl, a concentration camp survivor and world-respected author and psychotherapist, once commented on the impossibility of creating a successful life by one's self:

> Again and again I therefore admonish my students in Europe and America: Don't aim at success—the more you aim at it and make it a target, the more you are going to miss it. For success, like happiness, cannot be pursued; it must ensue, and it only does so as the unintended side effect of one's personal dedication to a cause greater than oneself or as the by-product of one's surrender to a person other than oneself.

Those of us who are Christians have long since discovered that Jesus Christ is the "one" who fulfills our deepest longings and ultimately positions us for success. Completion can only be found in the One who is complete.

Understanding the sovereignty of God makes me realize that I can trust Him. But I have to remind myself of that truth from time to time. I have to renew my mind to that reality when my emotions scream louder than the Word of God—when I believe my senses more than the Bible. But when all is settled and done, I know that God can be trusted.

The Scottish poet Robert Burns once wrote, "The best laid plans of mice and men often go astray." Well, to be exact, Burns wrote, "The best laid schemes o' mice an' men gang aft agley, an' lea'e us nought but grief an' pain for promis'd joy."[21] But since that doesn't make any sense to us, somebody translated it into English the way we speak it today. Your plans (and your poetry) may not always work out the way you intend, but you can be sure that the purpose of the Lord will ultimately prevail.

Three thousand years ago the words of the prophet Jeremiah conveyed God's intention toward us. Nothing has changed His heart since then. Nothing will.

"For I know the plans I have for you," declares the Lord, *"plans to prosper you and not to harm you, plans to give you hope and a future."*

—Jeremiah 29:11, NIV

Seeing Into Your Destiny

1. In what ways have you been searching after God? Have you drawn closer to Him?

2. How have you lost sight of the greatness of God and His desire to care for you?

3. Are you using the sovereignty of God as an excuse for passivity and inactivity?

4. What choices have you made recently without consulting God?

5. List the inner longings that you have been afraid to acknowledge. Why were you afraid to face them?

Profiles in Destiny

Profiles in Destiny

On a scorching summer day in the heart of the French and Indian War, the British army, led by George Washington, was sent to capture Fort Duquesne, the French stronghold on the Ohio River. In order to get there, they had to pass through dense forests, which put them at a decided disadvantage against the Indian warriors who were skilled in the art of stealth.

Nearing the end of their journey, an Indian war party ambushed them. Soldiers were dropping like flies, officers ran in panic, and soon Washington found himself to be the only officer alive. Gathering his courage, he led a perilous retreat without any place in which to take cover. Captain Washington had two horses shot from under him and later discovered four bullet holes in his uniform. It was a miraculous escape.

Fifteen years later, Washington was exploring territory in the Western Reserve when he encountered the same tribe that had attempted to take his life in the Battle of Monongahela. A council fire was built, and the chief relayed these words through an interpreter: "It was on the day when the white man's blood mixed with the streams of this forest that I first beheld this chief. I called to my young men and said, 'Mark yon tall and daring warrior. He is not of the redcoat tribe—he hath an Indian's wisdom, and his warriors fight as we do—himself alone is exposed. Quick, let your aim be certain, and he dies.'" But when the Indian warriors fired their rifles, which rarely missed, they were unable to hit Washington.

The old chief concluded his carefully chosen words: "Before I go there is something that bids me speak in the voice of prophecy: Listen! The Great Spirit protects that man and guides his destinies—he will become the chief of nations, and a people yet unborn will hail him as the founder of a mighty empire."

Chapter 3
Predestined to Be Awakened

Fate. Karma. Predestination. Providence. People have always wondered what the future holds and whether their lives have meaning and value. But the quest for destiny seems to have intensified in our generation. It's as if man has conquered the planet but still remains empty and unfulfilled. So we've turned our eyes from external achievement to internal fulfillment. But how can we have one without the other?

If, as some believe, there is no such thing as predestination, then our lives are only what we make of them in light of what we can coerce God into doing for us. If that be so, then the future is in our hands instead of God's. As Reese said in *The Terminator*, "There is no fate except what we make for ourselves." Born in 65 B.C., Horace, the most famous of all Latin lyric poets, declared, "*Carpe diem, quam minimum credula a postero.* Seize the day, and put the least possible trust in tomorrow." Nothing has changed our outlook on the future since then.

We are consumed with living *for* the moment rather than living *in* the moment and waiting with patient expectation for what tomorrow brings.

There are those who believe that the sovereignty of God leaves no room for human partnership and that our actions have no bearing on the future. God is viewed as an absentee landlord who has wound up the universe in much the same way a clockmaker might wind a clock before abandoning it to fate. Rather than seeing God as a loving Father who is committed to coaching us into greatness, He is perceived as an ambivalent neighbor disinterested in who we are and what we become. To those who hold this view, destiny is reduced to the social equivalent of the survival of the fittest. An examination of this almost indescribable phenomenon called *destiny* will help you to discern the purpose of your life and the role you play in finding and fulfilling your God-ordained future.

> **The future is the time when you'll wish you had done what you aren't doing now.**
>
> *—Unknown*

As we explore the intersection between God's sovereignty and human responsibility, we will see that a proper balance is vital to a healthy, productive Christian life. To deny predestination is to have an inadequate view of God—a view that eventually leads to humanistic thinking and the deification of man. On one hand, we run the risk of falling into *fatalism*—whatever will be will be. On the other hand, we run the risk of falling into *humanism*—the belief that our lives are the sum of the clever choices we have made. These are the two extremes I will seek to avoid while taking you on this journey toward a proper biblical balance.

When human responsibility is emphasized to the exclusion of predestination, even Christianity turns into legalism (religious humanism), without an appreciation for God's active power in our lives. If God's sovereignty is exclusively emphasized, Christianity turns into absolute determinism, losing the emphasis on obedience to God and service to others.

Dr. Norman Geisler, a self-described "moderate Calvinist," says:

> No one has ever demonstrated a contradiction between predestination and free choice. There is no irresolvable conflict being predetermined by an all-knowing God and it also being freely chosen by us.[1]

What Dr. Geisler fails to mention is that many have tried, albeit unsuccessfully. Even the Calvinistic *Westminster Confessions of Faith* (1646) makes this distinction when it states:

> Although in relation to the foreknowledge and decree of God, the first cause, all things come to pass immutably and infallibly, yet by the same providence He ordereth them to fall out according to the nature of second causes, either necessarily, freely or contingently.[2]

Walking the Razor's Edge

Let's look at two words—*predestinate* and *destiny*—and how they relate to the discovery and development of your purpose in life. Both words involve your past, present and future...your successes and failures...your hopes and dreams...your expectations and desires. The word *predestinate* involves everything God has planned for you in this life. But your destiny is determined by how much, or how little, you cooperate with God's plan.

The words *protithemi* ("to set beforehand") and *prohorize* ("to determine beforehand") are synonymous Greek terms. In English they translate into the verb form *predestinate* or the noun form *predestination*. A careful study of the Scriptures will reveal that both *events* and *people* are predestined. According to Paul's revelation *"all* things" are predestined according to the counsel of God's will.[3] Not just those things outside the scope of man's ability to intervene, or even the great events of world history, but all things, right down to the way we live every day. The scope of God's sovereignty is comprehensive and does not allow us to speculate that anything happens apart from the eternal plan of God. Simply stated, predestination is what God desires. What God desires He predestines. And what He predestines He makes certain to happen. Thus, everything is predestined.

Predestination is the divine determination of the way your life *should be* lived and the way your talents, gifts and abilities *should be* used. Predestination is the divine determination of the way your life will best glorify God and help others.

Does this sound like error-proof, predetermined engineering to you? Does predestination make history a series of "programmed" events and mankind merely robots? Far from it. If we were programmed to fulfill our destinies without ever lifting a hand to cooperate with the plan of God for our lives, there would be no need for faith and obedience—and both are major themes carefully woven throughout the tapestry of Scripture. The Christian life is a walk of faith on a path God has prepared.

> I do not believe in a fate that falls on men however they act; but I do believe in a fate that falls on them unless they act.

—*G. K. Chesterton*

Predestination by Permission

Predestination involves not only what God predetermines, but also what He allows by permission. For example, God foresees the sins of men and allows them as part of His eternal plan. But He doesn't cause us to sin. James, the disciple of Jesus, warned us of the danger of allowing our own moral weakness to determine our view of God. He said:

> Let no one say when he is tempted, "I am tempted by
> God"; for God cannot be tempted by evil, nor does He
> Himself tempt anyone. But each one is tempted when he is
> drawn away by his own desires and enticed. Then, when
> desire has conceived, it gives birth to sin.[4]

We all make choices in life that lead to certain actions, and
those actions have consequences. Thus, innocent children
suffer and the poor go hungry while the strong and the rich
seem to revel selfishly in their abundance. God allows, by permission, the presence of sin, even when it is contrary to His
original design for our lives.

David is an example of a man who made wrong choices and
whose sin had grave and long-lasting consequences. But who
knows what events might have transpired had David resisted the
fleshly impulses that night on the palace balcony?

Perhaps Uriah, Bathsheba's husband, would have been killed
in battle in the normal course of events, and David could have
met the grieving widow when he paid homage to those fallen in
battle. The outcome could have been the same without the
painful results of sin: They meet, they marry and they have a son
named Solomon who becomes king after David. I realize the
futility in this type of speculation, but it is something to consider.

Even though all that occurs is certain to occur according to
predestination, sinful deeds and even good acts of obedience are
not caused directly by God. Sin is permitted, while believers'
obedient acts are prompted and encouraged by the Holy Spirit
(they are also empowered by the Spirit, but the decision to obey
is truly that of the believer). So predestination, as it relates to
our destiny in life, involves what God determines and what God
allows.

We are now in what I call the "whitewaters of theology,"
and I'd rate the subject of predestination a "five" on the rapids
scale. This river is filled with rocks and debris, and our only
hope to navigate these rapids is to stay in the boat—keep

studying, keep thinking, keep praying and allow God to reveal the authority of His Word to us as He sees fit.

If we are to make peace with the subject of predestination, we have to set aside our fear of God controlling our lives, our fear that He won't make the right choices for us, our fear that He will take advantage of us. We have to surrender our stubborn resistance, our rugged American individualism and our need to become the quintessential "self-made person."

Absolute Power and Ordered Power

To understand predestination, it is necessary to distinguish between what theologians have come to call *absolute power* and *ordered power*. *Absolute power* is the overarching span of God's sovereign authority and is unlimited in its scope. Nothing exists in the universe that possesses the ability to resist what He desires and determines. According to absolute power, God could determine every action, right down to a mosquito landing on my nose in the middle of the night. If God wills for the mosquito to land on one's nose, then He just wills it, and it is done. According to absolute power, God is sovereignly in control, and His sovereign will is the only free will in the universe. Thus, humans cannot bring about what they want because their power is limited.

However, under the scope of absolute power, there is what theologians call *ordered power*. God has an overarching purpose for our lives, and within the framework of that purpose we are allowed to exercise the power of personal choice. Ordered power functions under the dome of divine covering, allowing us to make decisions using the resources God has given us to glorify Him. Under this dome of ordered power, God leaves room for limited free will (if you want to call it that).

I have always wrestled with the issue of free will, just as I struggle with the concept of people being free moral agents. Why? Because I have yet to meet a non-Christian who is either free or moral. Adam's legacy leaves each one of us as sinners firmly under the governing authority of the kingdom of darkness. Psalm 51 teaches us that we are shaped in iniquity, born in sin, captive to the power of this age and ruled by the enemy. Ephesians 2 reveals us as "dead" in our trespasses and sin. An honest review of your life before you came to Christ will remind you that you were neither free nor moral. Unregenerate man does not live in a spiritual vacuum, somewhere in between the God and the devil, where good and evil are equal choices. As Franky Schaeffer aptly pointed out in his prophetic work, *A Time for Anger: The Myth of Neutrality*, the neutral zone is but a figment of our imagination; it just doesn't exist in the real world.[5]

The realm of ordered power does have room for limited free will, if you still want to call it that. In his brilliant treatise *The Bondage of the Will*, Martin Luther writes of free will:

> But, if we do not like to leave out this term altogether (which would be most safe, and also most religious), we may, nevertheless, with a good conscience teach that it be used so far as to allow man a "Free will," not in respect of those that are above him, but in respect only of those things that are below him.[6]

Luther goes on to explain that people are free to use their possessions as they please, make and break relationships as they please, even eat dessert as they please, all the while acknowledging that it is within God's prerogative to overrule these things if He so desires. As a wise man once said, "Write your plans for life in pencil, and give God the eraser."

On the other hand, Luther continues:

> He [man] has, as to his goods and possessions, the right of using, acting and omitting, according to his "free will"; although, at the same time, that same "free will" is overruled by the free will of God alone, just as He pleases: but that God-ward, or in things that pertain unto salvation or damnation, he has no "free will," but is a captive, slave and servant, either to the will of God, or to the will of Satan. [7]

Five hundred years later, Bob Dylan growled out his version of Luther's brilliant treatise, "Well, it may be the devil or it may be the Lord, but you're gonna have to serve somebody, yes indeed."[8]

Luther seems to imply that the term "free will" means one thing where salvation is concerned and yet something entirely different where the matter of personal destiny is concerned. So as far as your salvation is concerned, Adam's sin left you neither free, moral nor in charge of your will. In the words of Paul, we were "entangled...with a yoke of bondage" when Christ found us and freed us.[9]

And now we have been given, as children of God, the power to make choices, in conjunction with the will of God, to bring forth the manifestation of our destiny in life. We have been given the privilege of colaboring with Christ as heirs and joint heirs. Predestination doesn't limit human responsibility where the matters of life are concerned. The grace of God consistently provides us with opportunities to become what we were destined to be, and by faith and obedience we capitalize on them.

In *What Luther Says in Knowledge of the Holy*, Martin Luther quoted:

> If God did not bless, not one hair, not a solitary wisp of straw would grow; but there would be an end to everything. At the same time, God wants me to take this stance: I would have nothing whatever if I did not plow and sow.

God does not want success to come without work. And yet
I am not to achieve it by my work.

When it comes to our own human destiny and to the matters
of life, God calls us to cooperate with Him in order to bring forth
everything that He has predetermined for us. And so we plow
and sow in the knowledge that He blesses and gives the increase.

> **Destiny is no matter of chance. It is a matter
> of choice: It is not a thing to be waited for; it
> is a thing to be achieved.**

—William Jennings Bryan

To See It Is to Be It

Our lives have been created for a purpose. When we choose to live
outside that purpose, trying to fill our lives with substitute plea-
sures, we find only emptiness. The reason many people struggle
with bondage, temptation and sin…the reason so many people
are captive to the powers of darkness…is because they have never
seen the beauty of their future. "Where there is no vision, the
people perish."[10] The New American Standard Version says,
"Where there is no vision, the people are unrestrained."

When you cannot see that God has a marvelous plan, an
intended future and a fulfilling destiny for your life, you lack
the internal power of restraint. For example, I've often noticed
that university students with clearly defined goals generally
apply themselves more diligently than those who are just going
for the experience. When I was a seminary student I attended
several classes with the son of a prominent denominational official. He slept through most classes, refused to study and failed
to make passing grades. When called upon publicly to answer a
theological question, he invariably responded to the professor,
"I believe whatever you believe. I'm just happy to be here."

To see the future is to prepare for it. Those with a clearly defined vision of the future are more likely to restrain themselves from actions that would impair their ability to reach that goal. I'm reminded of one lady who said that when her daughter and the daughter's boyfriend were in college, she prayed that their goals would be stronger than their hormones. Fortunately, they were. They graduated from college, married and are successful in their professions today.

> **In my experience, there is no such thing as "luck."**
>
> —*Obi-Wan Kenobi in* Star Wars

When we fail to see our place in the future, we tend to fill our lives with immediate gratification, as if that could give us a reason for living. But the present is never enough to satisfy the deepest longings of our heart. We need both history and destiny in order to live a balanced life. Contentment is found only in fulfilling the purpose for which we were born. Fulfillment is found in discovering and doing the perfect will of God all the days of our lives.

The apostle Paul was fully aware that both his history and his destiny were in God's hands. Perhaps that's why he opened his letter to the Colossians with this statement: "I, Paul, have been sent on special assignment by Christ as part of God's master plan." Then, in his prayer for these believers, he reminded them of their destiny: "The lines of purpose in your lives never grow slack, tightly tied as they are to your future...As you learn more and more how God works [His sovereignty], you will learn how to do *your* work [human responsibility]."[11]

What empowered Corrie ten Boom to endure those terrifying years in Nazi concentration camps? She knew her destiny was in God's hands, and she saw her place in the future.

How did Nelson Mandela survive imprisonment in

dehumanizing conditions and still retain the power of a positive mental attitude? He knew that his destiny was in God's hands, and he saw his place in the future.

Why are some people able to cope with seemingly unbearable circumstances, while others are crushed under the weight of despair? Those who cope successfully do so because they know their destiny is in God's hands, and they see their place in the future.

In his book *First Things First: To Live, to Love, to Learn, to Leave a Legacy*, author Stephen Covey writes about Viktor Frankl, the Austrian psychologist who survived the death camps of Nazi Germany. Frankl made a startling discovery about why some survived the horrible conditions, and some did not:

> He looked at several factors—health, vitality, family structure, intelligence, survival skills. Finally he concluded that none of these factors was primarily responsible. The single most significant factor, he realized, was a sense of future vision—the impelling conviction of those who were to survive that they had a mission to perform, some important work left to do. Survivors of POW camps in Vietnam and elsewhere have reported similar experiences: a compelling, future-oriented vision is the primary force that kept many of them alive.[12]

When Job's wife told him to curse God and die, he said, "Shall we indeed accept good from God, and shall we not accept adversity?"[13] In spite of his pain, confusion and frustration, He understood that the past, present and future all belong to the One who calls Himself the *Alpha and Omega*.

His Choices Are the Best Ones

We often tell our children, "You can be anything you want to be." We should be teaching them you cannot be anything *you* want to be—but you can be everything *God* wants you to be. Psalm 47 deals with the sovereignty of God in choosing our destiny. The psalmist says, "He will choose our inheritance for us, the excellence of Jacob whom He loves."[14]

Our struggle comes into play when our personal choices conflict with God's plan for our lives. As professing followers of Jesus
Christ, we should never presume that we have the right to choose
whom we marry, where we live and what we plan to do with our
lives. Ultimately, those choices are not up to us—they belong to
the sovereign Lord who rules over us. God chooses our inheritance for us. And when our choices conflict with His, we suffer.

We often see leaders guarding their positions jealously
because they have forgotten that those positions don't belong to
them but have been entrusted to them by God for His glory. If
God exalts someone over me or raises up someone who takes
my place, I must learn to surrender to His will. If I fight against
God, what value does my position hold outside of God's plan?
How do I know that God isn't raising up someone because He
has bigger plans for me? Even if God doesn't, the greater benefit is not the position I hold, but the fruit God produces
through my life for His eternal purposes. What could be
greater than to be chosen by God to touch someone's life who
will go where you cannot go and do what you cannot do? Who
led Billy Graham to Christ?

Consider this chain of God's providential events:

> A layman by the name of Edward Kimball led Dwight L.
> Moody to Christ. Dwight went on to be one of the greatest
> preachers of modern history. It was D. L. Moody who
> impacted F. B. Meyer, and Meyer touched Wilbur
> Chapman. Chapman partnered with Billy Sunday, and Billy
> Sunday had a major impact on Mordacai Ham. Mordacai
> Ham felt like a failure in his ministry and decided to quit.
> He felt burdened to do one more revival circuit. A sixteen-
> year-old boy with little interest in the revival was persuaded
> to go on one of the last services. That boy was named Billy
> Graham.
>
>   How many people would know who Mordacai Ham is?
> For that matter, how many people have ever heard of
> Edward Kimball? Did God use Edward Kimball to reach
> the masses? I guess it depends on how you look at it. God
> produced the fruit of his obedient labor. Edward Kimball is

as much of an heir to the fruit God produced as D. L. Moody and Billy Graham are. God is not interested in what you can do. God is interested in your obedience and faithfulness.[15]

Destiny is more than a conscious awareness of the destination; it is the lifelong journey toward the destination. Every ominous mountain, breathtaking valley, hairpin curve and wide-open stretch contain opportunities for growth and development along with the choice either to follow that segment of the journey or to go your own way stubbornly. Only when we fully surrender to the One who owns the map will we find true inner peace. Freedom from strife is found in resting in the knowledge that God has control of your life and will take greater care of you than you are capable of taking yourself.

What Determines Your Course?

You may have begun reading this book because of the frustration you have experienced in life. Perhaps you have even thought, *I could have been a success, but I never had the opportunity. I wasn't born into the right family. I didn't have the money to attend the best school. I missed too many opportunities, and now it's too late.* But when we measure success by faithfulness and obedience, it eliminates the frustration that is developed by using a false standard. Peace of mind is the result of acknowledging that there are certain issues in life over which you have absolutely no control. But God does.

Let's examine a few of the issues that tend to determine our course in life.

The family into which you were born

I once read about a man who was fifty-six years old and still trying to put himself up for adoption. Give it up! There comes a point in time when you have to resolve to move beyond the issues of abandonment, rejection, abuse and lack of proper parenting. To allow the unmet needs of your childhood to define the rest of your life is to miss the opportunity to become who God created you to be. A wise old man once told me, "Sometimes you have to be what you're looking for." Although you may not have been born into the best of circumstances, you can rise above them.

Your ethnicity

African or Irish, Swedish or German—God sovereignly chose your ethnic origins for you. Your destiny is inexplicably related to your identity. As I wrote in *The Image Maker*, "Mistaken identity always results in a wrong behavior. As a matter of fact, mistaken identity always results in a behavior out of accord with one's true identity. For the sake of illustration, let me describe it this way. If you can convince a man that he is a slave—when in fact he is a king by birth—then he will develop a slave mentality. In spite of who he is genetically, in spite of his heritability, he will never rise to the throne because he believed a lie concerning his identity."[16] Who you perceive yourself to be has immense bearing on what you accomplish in life.

Your gender

There is nothing more heartbreaking to witness in life than someone deceived into believing that their gender is not who they really are. Many people have been duped into believing that God mistakenly placed them in the wrong body. At the root of that lie are mistaken perceptions about the equal value of men and women. God made two separate categories of humanity as it relates to gender, and both are redemptively equal. Man and woman were created to co-rule creation as God's authorized representatives—both reflect different dimensions of His image.

The time in history in which you were born

I've often heard people say, "If only I had lived a hundred years ago." Or, "If only I could live a thousand years in the future." Quit wasting time daydreaming! Before you were created, God made full preparation for your arrival and for the fulfillment of your life's purpose. God took great care in placing you strategically in this moment in history—along with all of the necessary resources to succeed. Knowing that should produce great comfort in your life. People need you now. God needs you here. That's why He placed you in this moment in history.

Your natural talent and gifting

You have no choice over the natural talent or the natural gifting God has placed within you. You can neglect it, or you can refine it. But you were born with a proclivity toward certain things. Some people are good with numbers from their earliest moments of academic development. Others are gifted with artistic ability. A few are good at both. And some of us are good at neither. The simple reality is that God chooses our gifting, our talents and our abilities, and His choices are the best ones.

Learning to Trust the Driver

Are we forced to pursue the kind of life God has divinely chosen for us? Of course not—if you aren't interested in the incredible benefits that come with following His will. In other words, you cannot live with your choices and receive the benefits of His master plan. Decisions determine destiny. If you live life the way God designed for you to live, then you get the results that He foreordained for you. But if you live life your way, you get your own results.

God chooses your inheritance sovereignly, but you can yield to His choice or stubbornly insist on your own. The prodigal son is a perfect example of one who insisted on his own way. He demanded his inheritance and spent it as he chose. And when he had lost everything to his own mismanagement, he finally came to his senses.

Left to ourselves, we are bound to mismanage things of worth and value. That's why we need God. To follow God's plan for our lives involves total trust on our part. We can't do it halfway or halfheartedly. It's like a child learning to water-ski.

When I taught my sons to water-ski, it was a hysterical experience—on many different levels. For most of the summer they had watched other kids glide over the water and have a blast. All pumped up from watching their friends have the time of their young lives, they begged to give it a try. "C'mon, Dad, let's go!" they exclaimed, running to the boat on the day they were finally going to be able to try.

My youngest son, Tyler, was bursting with anticipation—until it came time to get out of the boat! After struggling into his life jacket, he awkwardly attempted to put the oversized skis on his feet when the gravity of the situation set in. His confidence dissolved into a puddle of stark fear! Try as I did, I could not persuade him into the water alone. Finally, I gave up and jumped in with him, and together we waited for the long awaited moment. As his mother pulled the boat into position to cruise into the calmest cove in the lake, he stared at it with the terror of *Jaws* in his eyes. It was one thing for him to stand on the boat deck with those skis on his feet—it was an entirely different matter of moving in the water. After all, it takes some practice to attach five-foot long pieces of fiberglass to your feet while maintaining your buoyancy and balance.

Tyler's teeth were chattering at machine gun rate. He was cold, nervous and clearly frightened at the intensity of the ride ahead of him. I wanted to laugh as I looked at him, but instead I coached him to take the challenge by saying, "You can do it! Just don't let go. The boat will pull you out of the water. Let it do the work; you just grab the rope and hang on. The life vest will keep you from drowning, the skis will keep you from sinking, but you can't water-ski unless you keep hold of the rope."

Then my "pastoral nature" took over, and I gave him some meaningful words of assurance: "What color flowers do you want at your funeral, just in case you don't survive?" I asked. He shot me a look that could wither steel girders.

The only way my sons could find out if they could ski

behind the boat was by hanging on to the rope. They couldn't prove that they could water-ski by putting on the life preserver and skis and walking around on the beach. They had to get into the water and grab hold of that rope and hang on. Until Tyler hung on to that rope, nothing of consequence could be proven. (By the way, I was so intent on teaching him to "pull up" that I forgot to tell him to let go when he got tired. I'm convinced that he still holds the record for the longest ski run in history!)

The same applies to our relationship with God. Unless you are willing to take action, get out of the presupposed security of the boat and risk grabbing hold of the rope, you will never know if you can trust Him. His trustworthiness will remain an incomplete and ineffective theological theory in your life instead of a powerful, life-changing dynamic.

Don't waste your life floating in the water, going nowhere, because you're afraid of hanging on to the rope, afraid of where the boat might take you. That's neither exciting nor fulfilling when you have been offered the opportunity to ski behind the Captain at breathtaking speeds, enjoying the thrill of the ride and taking comfort in the fact that He knows what's best for you. He knows what you need for the journey even better than you do. And if you will trust Him, He will make better choices for you than you can make for yourself. After all, He predestined you to be awakened.

Seeing Into Your Destiny

1. In your own words, explain the difference between the sovereignty of God and the responsibility of man.

2. Have you discovered the purpose of your life? What is it?

3. Picture yourself five years in the future. What do you see?

4. What choices have you recently allowed God to make for you? What were the end results?

5. List three ways you can increase your trust in God.

Profiles in Destiny

Profiles in Destiny

She taught children of privilege in a well-manicured neighborhood, which stood in sharp contrast to an adjacent slum area. Although the young teacher kept to herself and tried to avoid the neighboring area, one day she was drawn into it by the desperate cries of a pleading woman. There she found a destitute woman in dire need of medical care.

Seeing that the woman's condition was life threatening, the teacher rushed her to the nearest hospital. When the hospital staff observed that the sick woman could not possibly pay for her treatment, the teacher and the patient were told to wait. By then the situation was critical. The teacher realized that the woman was going to die without immediate medical attention. So she took her to another hospital, where they were again turned away. Conceding defeat, she finally took the dying woman to her own home where she passed away late that night.

In this defining moment of life, the young teacher decided that she would do everything within her power to prevent the suffering of anyone, anywhere. She decided to devote the rest of her life to easing the pain of those around her so that they could live or die with the dignity they deserve.

The city was Calcutta.

The woman was Teresa.

Chapter 4
History Belongs
to the Awakened

If you were to list the ten most "awakened" political leaders in the history of the twentieth century, Winston Churchill would be at the top of that list. Let's consider his story as an example of a man who embraced his destiny and changed the course of history during one of the darkest periods in the modern world.

In 1940 the world was in crisis. Adolph Hitler's Nazi Germany invaded Holland and France on its way to conquering the whole of Europe. The German advance appeared to be unstoppable. Duped by Hitler and discredited before all of Europe, Neville Chamberlain, the prime minister of England, resigned in disgrace. When he resigned, it was as if he threw up his hands and said, "Let's see if anyone else can handle this mess." The outcome of the war and the future of Europe would rest on the leadership of the new prime minister.

On May 10, 1940, King George VI summoned Winston Churchill to Buckingham Palace. The king quizzically stared at Churchill and said, "I suppose you don't know why I have sent for you?"

Adopting the king's mood, Churchill replied, "Sir, I simply couldn't imagine why."

The king laughed and said, "I want to ask you to form a government."[1]

Can you imagine the weight of responsibility that must have descended on Churchill at that moment? Yet he agreed. He met with political and military leaders and advisors, and they put together a coalition government.

Following his appointment Churchill wrote in his journal:

> As I went to bed at about 3 A.M., I was conscious of a profound sense of relief. At last I had the authority to give direction over the whole scene. I felt as if I were walking with destiny, and that all my past life had been but a preparation for this hour and for this trial...My warnings over the last six years had been so numerous, so detailed, and were now so terribly vindicated, that no one could gainsay me. I could not be reproached either for making the war or with want of preparation for it. I thought I knew a good deal about it all, and I was sure I should not fail. Therefore, although impatient for the morning, I slept soundly and had no need for cheering dreams. Facts are better than dreams.[2]

As I have read those words many times, they never cease to amaze me. How could this man feel a "profound sense of relief" on the night following his appointment to the most volatile position of leadership in a nation with an uncertain future? I certainly wouldn't have experienced any emotion even close to "relief"!

What caused Churchill to possess such confidence as he assumed leadership over an unprepared country, one that would stand against the greatest military machine that had ever existed to that point in history? What produced such raw determination in his life?

I believe Churchill was awakened to the purpose for which he had been born. For the first time in his life, he possessed the "authority to give direction over the whole scene." Rather than speculating from the sidelines, he was on the field giving orders to those who would shape the course of history alongside him. He recognized that his "authority" to act in a decisive manner was the result of this mystical quality called *destiny*. In one step of courage, he moved from quiet resolve into active purpose.

Winston Churchill hadn't lived an easy life. Though he was born in Blenheim Palace and reared in a life of luxury, he was severely lacking in academic initiative. There were times when he relied more on his natural talent than on the qualities of dedication and discipline. He hadn't always succeeded at the things he attempted. But in that one defining moment, standing before King George VI, he stepped forward and embraced his destiny. And through the efforts of one person, strategically placed and courageously living out his purpose, the spirit of Britain turned from despair to hope. Gradually the war was won—not only saving Britain from defeat but also, some would claim in retrospect, saving democracy as a form of government in the world. Winston Churchill shaped the course of history out of awareness of his own personal destiny.

> **No man is truly great who is great only in his own lifetime. The test of greatness is the page of history.**
>
> *—William Hazlitt*

Individuals who demonstrate extraordinary discipline, courage under fire, boldness in the face of uncertainty and perseverance against all odds are *history shapers*. We often look at those in leadership positions as larger-than-life-figures, somehow different from the rest of us. In world history we point to people like Abraham Lincoln, Winston Churchill and Mahatma Gandhi. We are inspired by legendary businesspeople like Bill Gates of Microsoft, Jack Welch of General Electric and Oprah Winfrey. In the political arena we esteem Nelson

Mandela and Anwar Sadat. Church history is also filled with men and women who changed the course of the world. Men like Martin Luther, John Calvin and Billy Graham demonstrated the qualities of exceptional leadership, and society is a better place because of their influence.

But what about the millions of men and women who have quietly shaped the course of history without recognition or reward? Are faithful mothers and fathers as important as the world-class leaders whose autobiographies line the shelves of our libraries? These are the nameless, faceless history shapers whose names may never appear on a magazine cover or in a history book, yet they profoundly affect our lives. History shapers, simply put, are those individuals who influence the lives of others for the better.

> A sub-clerk in the post office is the equal of a conqueror if consciousness is common to them.
>
> —*Albert Camus*

You were created to shape history. At some point in pursuit of your destiny, you must ask yourself, "What can I do in my generation to shape history—to influence the future to the glory of God?" The answer may be as simple as having a positive influence on the life of a child or as complex as dedicating your life to a twenty-year mission to alleviate human suffering. Regardless of your assignment, the outcome is to affect other people for the betterment of humankind.

The world is filled with unrecognized history shapers, potential history shapers and undeveloped history shapers. They pass us on the streets, stand next to us in checkout lines and sit next to us on pews without ever being recognized. They are the inconspicuous, remarkably ordinary people we encounter every day. They are mothers driving minivans, carpooling third graders to

Little League practice; teenagers working in grocery stores who don't take the time to bag the milk and bread separately; and underprivileged children getting dressed for school in the same tattered clothing day after day.

These potential history shapers are ordinary, unsuspecting planet sharers who have not discovered the purpose for which they were born. Some are educated; others are not. Some history shapers are born to power, wealth and prestige. Others come into this world in squalor, struggle with poverty and die in anonymity. There is no "one size fits all" description of history shapers. They share no common profile. They come from all walks of life and are formed from all temperaments. In the language of Scripture, they are motivated by different dimensions of "grace."[3] Some are prophetically motivated while others respond to the driving force of mercy, kindness and longsuffering.

Three Types of History Shapers

All history shapers will probably fit into one of three categories, regardless of education, opportunity, personal temperament or gift development.

Those who stumble into providence

The first type of history shapers are those ordinary people who seem to stumble into providence. Like the clueless detective in the 1970s' television program *Columbo*, they have a knack for showing up in the right place at the right time. Columbo never seemed to have a plan or know what he was doing—he just showed up in his trench coat, stuck out his bony little finger, waved it awkwardly and said, "I think I'm here to arrest somebody." Time and time again he bumbled into the solution.

History shapers of this type lead lives characterized by serendipity. They seem to have a gift for just being in the right place at the right time, and the right thing happens because they are there. These are the people who proved the maxim, "Great leaders are not born—they are cornered." At a moment of crisis or a strategic moment of need, they come stumbling onto the scene and somehow have the solution. These history shapers remind us of the sovereignty of God. He orders their steps and brings them into destiny in spite of themselves.

Gideon was this type of history shaper. He certainly hadn't set about to make a name for himself. He was hiding out by the winepress, afraid of the Midianites, afraid of the devastation in his nation and disappointed because there were no miracles in the nation as in times past. Yet when the angel of the Lord appeared to Gideon, he called Gideon "a mighty man of valor." This was, of course, ridiculous. Gideon was a coward, and he identified himself as such. Gideon was a man lathered with insecurities. But in spite of his devastated self-image, his personal insecurity and his uncertainty about the future, he stumbled into greatness because of one thing—the most important thing. He was chosen by God to change the world. The sovereign choosing of the Lord positioned him to become what he was destined to be.

Psalm 37 explains how this is possible: "The steps of a good man are ordered by the LORD, and He delights in his way."[4]

What we do in life echoes in eternity.

—*General Maximus Decimus Meridius in*
The Gladiator

Our feet are ordered by God, even when our eyes cannot see the path. Many times God leads us down pathways that we cannot identify, describe or understand—much less communicate to others. We just know that God is working in our lives and taking us somewhere. The Holy Spirit leads us even when we can't identify the destination.

I am convinced that I have stumbled into the will of God more times than I have intentionally walked into it. Sometimes, even though I was attempting to live according to wisdom, obey the Scripture, confess the Word and plan for greatness, I did not really see, nor could I clearly define, where God was taking me. But because I was following the Holy Spirit, He led me into opportunities to become who I was destined to be.

Many people will find their places in destiny because of the sovereign choosing of the Lord more than by their own personal plans. They are history shapers who seem to stumble into providence as God sovereignly lines up circumstances for His glory.

Those who sacrifice to fill a need

The second type of history shaper is the ordinary person who sacrifices to fill a need and in doing so changes the lives of others around him. Without any intention of impacting the world, these people respond to suffering humanity with compassion and end up changing lives and the course of history.

When Todd Beamer boarded United Airlines Flight 93 at Newark Airport on September 11, 2001, he never dreamed that he would be given the chance to shape history. Eighty minutes into the flight the airplane was taken over by hijackers, and the passengers found themselves the unwitting victims of a national terrorist plot. Refusing to "go quietly into the night," Todd, along with several other courageous passengers, decided to fight back. They stormed the cockpit, bringing the plane down in a remote field in Pennsylvania, saving countless lives—and perhaps even the Capitol Building. Weeks later, Lisa Beamer was interviewed by Stone Phillips regarding her final conversation with her husband from aboard that ill-fated flight.

"Why did he do it?" asked Stone.

"Todd was just an ordinary guy," Lisa replied. "He was extraordinary to me and to his family, but to the world he was ordinary. And like any ordinary guy getting on a plane that day in a business suit he was able to do extraordinary things."[5]

Todd Beamer and the heroic passengers of United Flight 93 were history shapers.

Mother Teresa was that type of an individual. She counted not her own life, even unto death, and in doing so, she changed the course of history for many people. When asked how she could continue day after day feeding the starving, wiping the fevered brow of a terminally ill AIDS patient or caring for the brokenhearted, she humbly replied, "In each of these faces I see the face of Christ in one of His more distressing disguises."

Matthew 26 records the story of the woman who took an alabaster flask of costly fragrant oil, broke it and anointed Jesus with it. The disciples, neither seeing the compassion of her heart nor identifying the moment of destiny, were incensed and indignant. They said to Jesus, "This fragrant oil might have been sold for much and given to the poor." But Jesus answered, "That's not what this is about. 'Wherever this gospel is preached in the whole world, what this woman has done will also be told as a memorial to her.'"[6] This woman was not calculating what effect her action would have on the future. She was concerned with the needs of that day, as compassion for Jesus moved her to minister to Him in worship. And in doing so, she became a history shaper.

Mark 15 introduces us to an oft-overlooked history shaper, Joseph of Arimathea, a Jewish councilman who watched the crucifixion of Jesus. Longing to see the kingdom of God, he could not stand by without taking part in the burial of the King. Following the death of Jesus, Joseph went to Pilate and requested the body be placed in his own personal tomb. In that one defining moment, Joseph of Arimathea became a history shaper.[7]

> **History is the record of an encounter between character and circumstance.**
>
> —*Donald Creighton*

The common thread linking each of these people is their willingness to sacrifice everything in order to meet a vital need in their generation. Modeling the character of Christ, their unrestrained compassion opened the door to destiny. At least ten times the Gospels mention where Jesus was "moved with compassion" for someone in need, and demonstrate how that compassion transformed itself into a miraculous healing touch.

The release of compassion often leads to the discovery of a ministry, as well as to great fulfillment. This kind of "destiny discovered" is not the result of a prophetically engineered plan of action, but the response of courageous living. Regardless of the situation—a terrorist attack, a hungry child, a homeless family, an AIDS patient, a hurting man or an abused woman—the need was the seed for the transformation of the history shaper and the situation. Few history shapers set out to be such; most step into destiny when they minister to others what God has placed within them.

Those who discover their calling and diligently prepare for it

The third type of history shaper is the person who discovers his or her calling and diligently prepares for it. The Scriptures are filled with the lives of remarkable men and women of courage who were willing to surrender their plans for life and embrace the greater purpose for living.

Daniel was such an individual. He was taken into captivity in Babylon in the summer of 605 B.C. and placed in the court of Nebuchadnezzar. In the early days of his captivity he made the decision to learn the language of Babylon without being nourished by the spirit of Babylon. He devoted himself to understanding the language of the culture so he could infiltrate and reform it. It was intentional. It was strategic. And Daniel changed the course of history.

Queen Esther prepared with all diligence when faced with her defining moment in history. Esther was facing the genocide of her people. But she knew there was something she could personally do about it—she needed to change the heart of the king in order to save her people. Esther assessed the situation and prepared accordingly. She didn't stroll casually into the throne room wearing grungy old sweatpants and dirty tennis shoes. The Bible shows us the picture of a woman carefully preparing to make the greatest possible impact on a heathen king. She bathed, using costly oils and the finest fragrances. She styled her hair attractively, applied her makeup skillfully and dressed in her royal garments. She knew that when she walked in before the king she had to touch his heart if she was to change the course of history. She intentionally, deliberately prepared with all diligence to save her people.

The characteristic shared by all three types of history shapers is this: When presented with crisis and opportunity, they respond rather than shrink back.

Any time we are faced with a crisis, we need to be aware that the crisis offers hidden opportunities. The word *crisis*, in Chinese, is made up of two symbols. The top character represents potential danger; the lower represents hidden opportunity. Together they convey the idea that every crisis presents the potential for both peril and providence. The results of a crisis depend on how we respond to it.

Every opportunity contains the possibility for tragedy, which is why many people let opportunities pass them by. I've often wondered how many businesses have never been built because someone was intimidated by the risk inherent within the opportunity. How many prophecies were never given because fear of getting up in front of the congregation was stronger than the prompting of the Holy Spirit? How many songs have never been sung because the songwriter feared criticism? How many books were never written because the author was unable to cope with rejection? How many opportunities for greatness have never been seized because, rather than focusing on the opportunity, people were overwhelmed by the hidden danger? The potential for failure is inherent in every possibility we encounter in life. Let's face it—marriage is a risky business. Having children is certainly a risky proposition, given the dangerous climate of today's world. But the outcome is worth the risk in every situation.

Characteristics of History Shapers

We live in an extraordinary time in the history of the world. We live at a time when mankind is making dynamic breakthroughs that are setting the stage for an unprecedented future. Less than one hundred years ago our great-grandparents lived in a world without automobiles, airplanes and satellite technology. As the twenty-first century begins we are witnessing scientific and technological feats that they would have considered impossible—if not downright pure fantasy. In the past century alone we witnessed startling breakthroughs in technology, medicine and global communications. We landed on other planets, put a space station in orbit, launched global satellite communications, grew test-tube babies and cloned animals.

And the best is yet to come! As the third millennium unfolds, man is in the process of discovering how to assume control over matter, develop new energy sources, cure what were previously considered to be incurable diseases and tap new resources in nature. None of these remarkable accomplishments will be completed without the dedication of men and women committed to progress.

Having spent my life studying the character of history shapers, I have discovered several common threads that consistently appear in the tapestry of their lives. These fibers are woven throughout their being, thus forming the patterns of greatness. To ignore them is to miss what separates a history shaper from a daydreamer.

History shapers foresee the future while managing the present.

It's human nature to look to the future. Man has always studied the skies for clues about what lies ahead. Our hunter/gatherer forebears honed an invisible sense of where to find the best game and the finest berries. Wise leaders observed the tides of restlessness sweeping their tribes and devised proclamations to stay ahead of the group. Divination and prophecy were legitimate and revered skills in ancient times. A few correct hits assured the ancient futurist a favored place closest to the king. In fact, knowing the future has always been one of the quickest routes to power.

Now millennium fever is making futurism highly fashionable. Sometimes it seems as if almost everyone has a take on where we are heading. Yet the most important thing about all the scenario building and future tripping is that it opens a door for each of us to begin tuning into our personal sense of what lies ahead. Abraham Lincoln once said, "If we know where we are and something about how we got there, we might see where we are trending—and if the outcomes that lie naturally in our course are acceptable, to make timely change."

Awakening our ability to see unfolding patterns may be the most important psychological skill we can cultivate. With the right keys every individual, business and community have the opportunity to enter a world of unprecedented renewal. Yet it is pointless unless we understand the nature of the journey we are undertaking and rewrite the close of the story. Otherwise, we could have an ending that would undermine any vision we might have of the future.

Foresight involves an attitude of the heart *and* latitude of the mind. It is the unapologetic revelation of your hopes and dreams balanced with your need to carefully weigh the odds. It opens up new horizons and provokes deep insecurities. It is the embodiment of dedication and intuition. As a result, you will find yourself, at once, believing for greater things and carefully analyzing the risks.

In his book *Leadership Is an Art*, Max Dupree stated, "The art of leadership dwells a good deal in the future, providing for the future of the organization, in planting and growing other leaders who will look to the future beyond their own."[8] The first requirement of leadership is the ability to envision the future destination of any enterprise. Jesus also described that necessary quality as the character of a disciple. In His call to radical discipleship He challenges us to count the cost and to determine in advance whether we are willing to embrace the mission.[9]

In his book *Transforming Leadership*, Leighton Ford said, "History is filled with instances when powerful leaders have failed to meet the challenge of the future."[10] Careless leaders make long-range plans as if the future is an extension of the present—when it isn't. The future is a world of its own. It's a clean slate, an unwritten book or an uncomposed song. It's an opportunity to create what does not currently exist. Every history shaper faces the challenge of maintaining a vision for the future while dealing with the mundane of the present. The temptation is to detach mentally and emotionally from challenges we currently face in order to quickly access the hopes we harbor for tomorrow.

But to detach from the present is to become disqualified from the future. "Why?" you ask. Because it will take every lesson we have learned and every experience we have processed through to position us properly for what the future holds.

Foresight is the central ethic of leadership.

— Robert Greenleaf

History is filled with leaders who did long-range planning as if the future were an extension of the present—rather than a world of its own. Consider some of the world's worst predictions:

- In 1773 King George II said that the American colonies had little stomach for revolution.

- In 1876 Western Union sent this internal memo: "This telephone has too many shortcomings to be seriously considered as a means of communication. The device is inherently of no value to us."

- In 1912 an official of the White Star Line, speaking of the firm's newly built flagship, the *Titanic*, declared that the ship was unsinkable.

- In 1939 the *New York Times* said the problem with TV was that people had to glue their eyes to a screen and that the average American wouldn't have time for it.

- In 1943 Thomas Watson, chairman of IBM, said, "I think there is a world market for maybe five computers."

- With over fifty foreign cars already on sale here, the Japanese auto industry isn't likely to carve out a big slice of the U.S. market.

- In 1977 Ken Olson, president, chairman and founder of Digital Equipment Corp., said, "There is no reason anyone would want a computer in their home."

- In 1962 Decca Recording Company rejected the Beatles, saying, "We don't like their sound, and guitar music is on the way out."

- In 1981 Bill Gates said, "Six hundred forty kilobytes of memory ought to be enough for anybody."

- In 1982 IBM said, "One hundred million dollars is way too much to pay for Microsoft."[11]

Today we laugh at these predictions and then make the same mistake ourselves by predicting the future based on the experience of the present or the pain of the past. Making the choice to attach yourself prophetically to the future is empowering because it offers you the opportunity for a new beginning. As one prophetic speaker said to his audience, "I see you somewhere in the future, and you look much better than you look right now!"

History shapers speak the language of the future.

There is an interesting map on display in the British Museum in London. It's an old mariner's chart, drawn in 1525, outlining the North American coastline and adjacent waters. The cartographer made some intriguing notations on areas of the map that represented regions not yet explored. He wrote: "Here be giants," "Here be fiery scorpions," and "Here be dragons." Eventually, the map came into the possession of Sir John Franklin, a British explorer in the early 1800s. Scratching out the fearful inscriptions, he wrote these words across the map: "Here is God."

Martin Luther King Jr. faced the grim reality of the present when he considered the plight of his fellow African Americans. But he spoke the language of the future when he boldly declared to the nation, "I have a dream..." And that dream inspired not only his own people, but also people everywhere, to work toward true freedom.

The language of the future is the expression of faith. Romans 4, speaking of the faith of Abraham, says that Abraham "believed—God, who...*calls those things which do not exist as though they did.*"[12] Abraham invested personal faith in the God who controls the future. He readily embraced the language of the future—the language of faith. The language of the future is not the language of lack, scarcity or insufficiency. It never declares, "We are grasshoppers in our own sight." The vocabulary of faith does not contain the words: "I'm too young, too old, too uneducated, too ethnic, too unprepared or too ill equipped." Such statements are the language of the present and of the past—the language of unbelief. The language of the future is the language of faith.

> Now faith is the substance of things hoped for [the future], the evidence of things not seen [the future]. For by it [faith] the elders obtained a good testimony. By faith we understand that the worlds were framed by the word of God, so that the things which are seen were not made of things which are visible.[13]

Before anything existed in the created order, God spoke the language of the future and said, "Let there be." The voice of faith is the language of creation.

> By faith Noah, being divinely warned of things not seen [the future], moved with godly fear, prepared an ark for the saving of his household, by which he condemned the world and became heir of the righteousness which is according to faith. By faith Abraham obeyed when he was called to go

out to the place which he would receive as an inheritance. And he went out, not knowing where he was going [not knowing the future].[14]

These Old Testament history shapers spoke the language of faith, calling the future into manifestation. Fearlessly they tapped into the power of the age to come and lived the future in the present. Welcome to prophetic living. God has called us to be prophetic in the sense that we hear His voice, we feel His heart and then we declare, "Your kingdom come. Your will be done on earth as it is in heaven."[15]

History shapers create what the future does not seem to contain.

Long before the Internet rocketed onto the scene of the late twentieth century, long before satellite technology linked the whole earth together in one technological protocol, the telephone was the standard of local, national and global communication. When Samuel Morris invented the telephone, he recognized that he was but an instrument of God. The first words spoken over this new invention were, "Look what God has done."

> **It is difficult to say what is impossible, for the dream of yesterday is the hope of today and the reality of tomorrow.**
>
> —*Robert H. Goddard*

History shapers don't wait passively for the future to reveal itself. They create the future by passionate devotion to bringing God's very best into their lives, character, relationships, career, mission, talents and giftings.

God made us in His image so that we could be creators in relationship with Him.[16] In the Hebrew Scriptures, the verb for "create," *bara*, is used fifty-four times. While God is usually the subject of the verb, on six occasions this word is used to describe human action.[17] Creativity is a prophetic action. In Ezekiel, God commands the prophet to create—to bring into existence what does not presently exist.[18] History shapers create the future when it does not seem to contain what God has put in their heart.

One of the great history shapers of the twentieth century, George Washington Carver, boldly said, "Man, who needed a purpose, a mission, to keep him alive, had one. He could be... God's coworker..." What a remarkable statement! But what makes those words even more remarkable is the life that Carver lived. Born to a slave during the Civil War, he faced a mountain of obstacles in his lifetime. He lived in a dark period of history and fought his own personal battles with racism, prejudice, poverty and lack of opportunity. Yet he refused to quit in the face of adversity. He had a revelation. He knew he had a purpose. He was awakened to the fact that God was inviting him to be His coworker.

Seeing the depletion of the soil due to generations of cotton farming, Carver began to focus on other crops that would revitalize the soil and free the economy from its dependence on cotton. In the face of economic disaster from the boll weevil plague, farmers began to follow Carver's advice and plant peanuts and sweet potatoes. However, there was no available market for these products, so Carver set out to create one. His scientific discoveries were an extension of his life of faith. Every morning he walked through his laboratory gardens asking God to unlock the secrets of His creation.

Out of his passionate devotion to create the future, Carver created over three hundred products from the peanut, ranging from soap to cosmetics to linoleum.

George Washington Carver spoke the language of the future and created what the future did not seem to contain.

History shapers perform the possible and believe for the impossible.

History shapers make peace with the paradoxes of the

kingdom. They learn to distinguish between their role and God's role in the discovery and development of their destiny. They learn to "do what their hand finds to do with all their might," while also recognizing that "it's not by might, nor by power, but by the Spirit of the Lord." They change what they can and leave the rest to God.

Here's some great advice concerning your responsibility in finding and fulfilling your destiny. If you can change it, change it! If you can build it, build it! If you can buy it, buy it! If you can be a part of making it happen, do it. And if you can't, then believe God to take you beyond the limitations of your life into the resources of the kingdom.

History shapers refuse to settle for the status quo.

Deep within the history shaper is the knowledge that the Garden of Eden was not the final destination for man—it was merely the starting place. When God created our original parents, Adam and Eve, He commissioned them to manage the planet on His behalf.[19] This commission, otherwise known as the "Dominion Mandate," became the driving force behind all progress in Eden. As a result of Adam's stewardship, the animals were named, the Garden was tended and preparation was made to bring the earth under the government of God.[20] But sin broke the momentum.

Not only did man's transgression place him at a disadvantage against the powerful undercurrents of sin and shame working in the planet, but it also broke his spirit. His life lost its original meaning and purpose. Rather than dominating the planet on God's behalf, Adam settled into the mundane, working by the sweat of his brow. The days, weeks, months and years rolled into one long treadmill of futility. He accepted the status quo without any hope for change.

Guy Chevreau once said, "*Status quo* is Latin for 'what a fine mess we've gotten ourselves into.'"[21] And so it is. Our failure to enter the portal of destiny often leaves us with the bitter aftertaste of opportunity missed. The choice we face is a simple one—to advance or retreat, to reach or settle, to conquer or yield. History shapers are those whose grasp exceeds their reach. They realize that to change the course of history is to create a better world for others to dwell in.

It's a great life if you don't weaken.

—*John Buchan (Mr. Standfast)*

Let's end this chapter one month after we began it. On June 4, 1940, less than one month after he became the prime minister of England, Winston Churchill reported to the House of Commons on the status of the war. Little progress had been made. Hope was bleak; fear was rampant. Yet, during some of the darkest days of World War II, Prime Minister Winston Churchill gave one of the greatest speeches in history. In it he said:

> We shall defend our island whatever the cost may be; we shall fight on the beaches; we shall fight in the fields; we shall fight in the streets; and we shall fight on the hill. We shall never surrender, and if this island were subjugated and starving, our empire on the seas would carry on the struggle until in God's good time the New World with all its power and might steps forth to the rescue and liberation of the old.

Years later, when asked to share the secret of his success as the Prime Minister of Great Britain, the boy from Blenheim Palace strode purposefully to the podium, pulled himself up to his full height and said, "Never give in, never, never, never, never—in nothing great or small, large or petty—never give in except to convictions of honor and good sense." Winston Churchill's awareness of destiny enabled him to shape world history, and mankind is better for it.

What are you doing to shape the world in which you live?

Seeing Into Your Destiny

1. What are the three types of history shapers? Which type best describes you?

2. List three ways you are actively preparing for your future.

3. Have you ever failed to plan for an opportunity? How? What did you do to correct your mistake?

4. Are your words filled with faith and hope or doubt and unbelief? Make the decision to align your words with the will of God for your life.

5. In what ways have you settled for the status quo? What are you doing to break free?

Section II

The Discovery

Awakened
to
Destiny

Profiles in Destiny

Profiles in Destiny.

Harriet was a preacher's kid. Actually, she was the daughter of Lyman Beecher, a respected theologian and the president of Lane Theological Seminary in Cincinnati, Ohio. In a day when the clergy was the most respected of all occupations, Lyman was the most famous orator in America. But little Harriet was to have the greatest impact on the nation.

As a child growing up in the mid-nineteenth century, Harriet was appalled by the slavery that flourished across the Ohio River in Kentucky. Outraged by this and the passage of the oppressive Fugitive Slave Act of 1850, she began writing a novel based upon a vision she had in church one Sunday morning. By dramatizing the plight of slaves through easily understood and highly sympathetic characters, Harriet provoked the conscience of the North and brought new respectability to the cause of abolition.

Her captivating story first appeared in serial form in the abolitionist journal, *National Era*. In January of 1852, one year after Harriet's vision, her story was released as a book and sold over three hundred fifty thousand copies within the first year. Never has a single novel had such an effect on a nation and its course in history as did this one. By 1860 it had been translated into twenty languages and produced as a play on countless stages in the United States and abroad.

So great was the impact of her book that when President Abraham Lincoln met her he said, "Why, Mrs. Stowe, right glad to see you! So you're the little woman who wrote the book that made this great war." That war brought about the realization of Harriet's vision, which was the freedom of over three million slaves.

The book that captured President Lincoln's and the rest of the nation's attention was Harriet Beecher Stowe's *Uncle Tom's Cabin*.

Chapter 5
Your Identity
Is Your Destiny

What matters, therefore, is not the meaning of life in general, but rather the specific meaning of a person's life at a given moment.

—Viktor Frankl

Many years ago there lived a dearly beloved Jewish sage named Rabbi Zsuya. He was renowned throughout the world for his gifted insights as a scholar, teacher and compassionate leader. When the time came for Rabbi Zsuya to leave this world, his students gathered at his bedside. During an emotional moment, the rabbi began to weep.

"Why are you crying, Rabbi?" asked one of the disciples. "If anyone is assured of a place in heaven, it is you. You are one of the greatest and most revered teachers in the world!" Rabbi Zsuya turned his head slightly toward the one who spoke and looked him in the eye. His gaze was piercing, as one who could see into the heart of his student.

"I will tell you why I weep," the rabbi replied. "If, when I approach the gates of heaven, the angel who meets me asks, 'Why were you not a Moses?' I shall answer with conviction, 'Because I was not born to be a Moses.' And if the angel challenges me, 'But neither did you perform the feats of Elijah,' I shall firmly respond, 'My mission was not the same one that Elijah was sent to accomplish.' But there is one question I fear being unable to answer," the rabbi concluded. In unison the students asked what that question could be. With deep weariness in his voice the wise old rabbi said, "I fear being asked, 'Why were you not a Rabbi Zsuya?'"

This allegory speaks to the deepest issue of our lives. Your greatest concern should not be over why you are not a Billy Graham, Mother Teresa or William Gates III. Your greatest interest should center on simply being who God created you to be. God created you to be a unique, exceptional, inimitable, one-of-a-kind individual. Each of us is as different as a snowflake, irreplaceable and unable to be replicated.

When asked what was most worthy of awe and wonder in this theater of the world, Abdala the Saracen answered, "There is nothing to see more wonderful than man!" Saint Augustine, bishop of Hippo, observed one of the great tragedies of life to be when "men go forth to wonder at the heights of the mountains, the huge waves of sea, the broad flow of rivers, the vast compass of the ocean, the courses of the stars, and they pass by themselves without wondering."

I am convinced that this generation will never settle the mystery of God as long as we ignore the mystery of man. To paraphrase the words of John the Beloved, "If you fail to acknowledge and embrace your brother whom you have seen, how can you acknowledge and embrace God whom you have not seen?"[1] It is our spiritual blindness to the intrinsic worth of every human, Christian and non-Christian, that prevents us from seeing the beauty and power of the Creator. To turn a blind eye to the wonder of man is to ignore the One in whose image we have been made.

Let's consider for a moment what it means to be human. The psalmist David poetically described man as being "fearfully and wonderfully made."[2] Our Father made you distinct—from the genetic code programmed into your DNA to the number of hairs on your head. Out of six billion inhabitants of Planet

Earth you are the only one with your unique set of fingerprints. With the birth of our first son, Judith and I sat quietly for hours counting and recounting fragile fingers and tiny toes. Strangely enough, of all the wonders contained in this bundle of joy, I was intrigued the most with the delicate little fingernails replicating my own. That initial astonishment did not lessen with the birth of our second son, and finally the third. Born to a brown-haired father and a blond mother, we produced one redhead, one blond and one with dark brown hair!

> **Before we can become fully divine, we must become fully human.**
>
> —*St. Ignatius*

There is no scientific achievement by man that even compares to the creation of man. We were created as the crowning achievement of all creation. I am constantly amazed at the complexity of the human design.

Consider this. Cells are the basic building blocks of life. Every living thing is comprised of cells—humans, animals, plants and minerals. The human body, for example, contains about one hundred trillion cells, and each cell contains as much information as ninety volumes of the *Encyclopedia Britannica*. Yet each cell is small enough that five million red blood cells and five million white blood cells would fit on the head of a straight pin. Some cells are assigned the task of manufacturing and maintaining the material that forms bone and cartilage, while others form skin, muscles and internal organs.

The structure of the human body is composed of DNA, which consists of an estimated three billion pairs of nucleotides, called base pairs, arranged like the steps of a twisting ladder. Along the helical ladder, these pairs occur in a pattern otherwise known as a sequence. They are marked off by clusters of hundreds of thousands—in some cases millions—of base pairs, which constitute genes. Geneticists have determined that each cell contains a maximum of one hundred thousand genes. DNA is so finely constructed and compressed that all of the cells contained within a human body could fit into a half-inch square cube; yet if the DNA were joined together end to end, the strand would stretch around the earth more than three million times.

As astonishing as the human body is, it is eclipsed by the intricacy of the brain. A single human neuron has limited capabilities, but if you place ten billion neurons with sixty trillion synapses together in the cerebral cortex, then an individual will have a brain that thinks and directs neurological signals to the entire human body.

Now you can more fully understand why the psalmist proclaimed us to be fearfully and wonderfully made. Man is God's greatest creative achievement.

Designed for Distinction

Painted on the ceiling of the Sistine Chapel is one of the most fascinating works of the Italian Renaissance. The Sistine Chapel, built according to the exact dimensions of the Temple of Solomon, is a work of art itself, and it is the perfect setting for the most noted work of Michelangelo Buonarroti. If you're fortunate enough to be alone in the Chapel, you might want to consider lying down on the cold, stone floor just to study the ceiling before moving on to the next painting. It's hard for me to stand still for long when they all seem to be calling my name. Of the nine epic scenes depicted from the Book of Genesis, I am captivated most by the way the famed artist envisioned the serenity of man as he was created in the image of God.

There is a virginal quality about the expression on Adam's face as he responds to the Creator with a mixture of innocence, trust and loving submission in his eyes. His wrist is bent, not as a sign of effeminacy as some might misinterpret, but as an act of subservience to His Maker. Adam's loving gaze is met by the strength of God's firm resolve as the Creator purposefully extends His finger, making contact with the one He has formed in His image.

There's another picture that holds my fascination as well. It sits on the cluttered credenza behind my writing desk. Surrounded by stacks of sermon files, unfinished correspondence and cluttered research material, I occasionally catch a glimpse of it as I impatiently rummage around looking for some long-lost item. It is my image, sketched in pencil and framed by black construction paper glued onto cardboard. The likeness is fairly good—at least for an eleven-year-old artist—but that is not what holds my attention. It's my love for the author. He sketched me with pride and did his best to capture my dignity.

Genesis 1 snaps the shutter on a picture of almighty God as He crafts man with pride and forms him with dignity.[3] On the sixth day of Creation, after having formed everything else that exists in the created order, God formed man.

Have you ever considered the three characteristics that are unique about the creation of man?

Man was created from the dust of the earth by the hand of God. God used the very lowest substance of the planet to form the highest of His creation. There is no indication that the plants and animals were created through the touch of God. All indication puts them as being simply commanded into existence. But man was fashioned from creation in that God took the dust of the earth and with his own hands formed man. He is seen as the Master Potter creating His greatest masterpiece, and, when finished, he gave it life. God took great care to fashion man with His own hands—man is the hand-made creation of almighty God. Man carries the special touch of the Creator.

Man was created in the image of God. What does it mean to be created in the image of God? It means that the Creator generously allowed humankind to share in some of His very own characteristics. As Herman Bavinck once stated, "Man does not simply bear or have the image of God; he is the image of God."[4] Man is not only flesh and bone; he is soul and spirit. In essence, the intention is that while we are not God, or gods, we are to mirror God's qualities and attributes. Those around us are to see Him in us.

God breathed into man's nostrils the breath of life. That one action speaks volumes of the closeness God desired to have with man. Once he had fashioned man, God then gave man a part of Himself, the breath of life from His own presence. Life was given to man through contact with the very presence of God.

> **Consider how Christ works and labors for me in all creatures upon the face of the earth.**
>
> —*St. Ignatius*

Why are these three things significant to our understanding of God and man's relationship to Him? These divine actions reveal the divine intention—God's desire to have a special relationship with man. Man's creation was on a higher level than the animals and plants. The Scriptures describe the creation of many plants and animals, indicating multiples of each kind, but only one man and one woman—and the woman was created from man.

Everything about the creation of man develops the biblical theme of God's love for man. It was a relationship that, from the beginning, involved God touching and caring for man as a parent cares for a child. He was willing to hold man in his arms, converse with him, nurture him and allow man to experience His presence in every way—total involvement. All of creation was to benefit man, and man was to care for it.

Designed for Dignity

If there is such a thing as a "manifesto" of the Italian Renaissance, Pico della Mirandola's "Oration on the Dignity of Man" is it; no other work more forcefully, eloquently or thoroughly remaps the human landscape to center all attention on human capacity and the human perspective. Surrounded by the carefully crafted images of enlightenment, it must have been difficult to see man in his proper position—a place of dignity and dependence. The dangerous trap Mirandola falls into, and the one we must avoid, is the overestimation of man apart from union with Christ. Fallen man, at best, is a faint image of his original glory in the Garden of Eden. As I wrote in *The Image Maker*:

> The primary thought that impresses me as I carefully con-sider the language of Genesis 1 is that man was created in the image and likeness of God. The word translated as "image" is *tselem*; the word translated as "likeness" is *demuth*. In the Hebrew language there is no conjunction between the two expressions; the text simply states, "Let us make man in our image, after our likeness." The Septuagint and the Vulgate, however, insert the word *and* between the two words, leaving us with the impression that "image" and "likeness" refer to two different things. My personal belief is that even though these two words appear to be synonyms, there are some subtle, but significant dif-ferences between them...Although the words *image* and *likeness* are occasionally used interchangeably, when used together they reveal a broader picture of the original design of man...fallen man still possesses the image of God, but he desperately needs the atoning work of Redemption to restore him back to the likeness of God that he expressed before the Fall. This distinction enables me to see the basic worth of all men while also recognizing the special nature of redeemed man. Through the power of the new birth experience, Jesus Christ restores the likeness of God the Father back to fallen man.[5]

Rather than focusing any further on the image of fallen man, I want us to consider what man has now become through his rela-tionship to Jesus Christ, for that is the true essence of Christianity. The gospel is not a story about an abstract God sending His representative Son to redeem a nameless, faceless people—it is the biography of redeemed man. You are a central character in the drama of redemption. I am a vital figure in the greatest love story of all times. Without you and me, redemption

was a frustrated mission. It took the response of man to fulfill
God's original intention—to have a family of sons and daughters
who would live and move and find their being in Him.[6]

You are the love child of the King of the universe.

You have royal blood flowing through your veins.

You are unconditionally loved.

You are irrevocably accepted.

You are eternally blessed.

You have been given a unique combination of talents and
experiences.

Designed for Greatness

You hold the exclusive patent on your personal identity. Even
though you may have the exact same gifts, talents and abilities
that millions of other people in the world possess, your distinc-
tiveness lies in your unique combination of temperament,
talent, insight, character and experience.

Millions of people may be gifted with the same talent as you,
but they won't have the same temperament and experience.
Others may have the same temperament as you, but their
gifting lies in other areas. You may share the same spiritual or
motivational gifts as many others, but your mix of insight, personality and character will make your life and ministry unique.
The distinctive blend of what may seem to be common qualities
is what makes you exceptional. What God has assigned you to
accomplish in life cannot be compared to others because it is
the by-product of your uniqueness. And with all of us working
together we have the potential to steward our world to the glory
of God.

You have been fashioned a particular way—spiritually, physically, emotionally, psychologically, intellectually, relationally
and environmentally—to fulfill a certain role in life. All of this
is by divine design. The Creator intrinsically connected our
potential for productivity to the identity that He sovereignly
chose for us. He shaped you a unique way to fulfill a certain

role, to perform a specific task and to produce precise results. As you fulfill your role in this vast world, your life becomes the evidence of the existence of the Great Designer of the Universe.

To envy another's mission or to attempt to reproduce someone else's assignment is to settle for less than what God has chosen you to accomplish. In fact, to accept someone else's mission is to condescend to a life that is not your own and to experience an outcome that was not designed for you. Your identity is your destiny. The two are inseparable. Always have been. Always will be.

> Lionel, if you don't watch out, you're going to go from being a "has been" to a "would be" without every having been an "is."

> —*Mrs. Jefferson in* The Jeffersons

The Law of Being

The past two decades have shown that the world has shifted into perpetual high gear and taken on such a frenetic pace that there seems to be little time to contemplate the actions we are rushing to take. We have become human *doings* rather than human *beings*, which may be why we are dying spiritually of hardening of the *oughteries*. Were William Shakespeare writing prose today, he might be tempted to revise what is arguably his best-known line to read, "To *do* or not to *do*, that is the question." Ask someone, "Who are you?", and the chances are he will respond by listing his activities rather than his identity.

- "I'm a teacher."
- "I'm a doctor."
- "I'm a minister."
- "I'm a father."
- "I'm a supervisor."

After pastoring two churches over the course of fifteen years, I experienced an identity crisis of sorts. I found myself in between pastorates for a six-month period while I wrote, conducted seminars and spoke in conferences. But I wasn't actively pastoring. One day shortly after we arrived in our community, Tyler, my youngest son, can home from the third grade with a question. *"Dad, what are you now?"* he asked. I groped for an answer, rambling on about what I was doing. His eyes glazed over. Tyler was looking for a noun—pastor, lawyer, doctor, teacher—and all I could give him was a string of participles: *doing this* and *doing that*. For a few months I struggled with the way in which transition was refining and even redefining my life. I've coached others through this same struggle.

- "I don't even know who I am any more without my career."

- "How can I really serve God without a title or a position?"

- "If I'm not his wife, who am I?"

- "With our last child out of the 'nest,' I don't know what to do with myself."

The law of being defines us as human *beings*—not human *doings*. Life is something we *live*, not something we *do*. Think about that simple statement for a moment. Once upon a time we used to live life at an unhurried pace, allowing the future to take care of itself. But the past two decades have shown me that my world has somehow shifted into perpetual high gear and taken on such a frenzied pace that there seems scant time left anymore to schedule in a breath, let alone contemplate the implications of *doing* vs. *being*. No longer is there time for weekend picnics planned spontaneously on Saturday morning or dropping by the neighbor's house for coffee and conversation. Rather, a mountain of responsibilities and expectations keep us artfully enmeshed in the dance of doing until, exhausted, we fall off into a fitful slumber imitating sleep, filled with thoughts of what *doings* the next day will demand! There was a time when we were at peace with the length of time it takes to plant a harvest and reap a crop; now we are depleting the soil by trying to get multiple harvests in one year.

Likewise, when it comes to our inner sense of being, we strive to *do* what we have not taken the time to *become*. Scripture asks, "Does a spring send forth fresh water and bitter from the same opening...No spring yields both salt water and fresh."[7] We should ask ourselves, "Can we live as human doings and still produce a sense of inner well-being?" The answer to both questions is *no*!

What Is the Purpose of Being?

Hugh Morehead, chairman of the Department of Philosophy at Northeastern University, spent forty-five years of his life writing to famous philosophers, scientists and authors and asking them, "What is the purpose of life?" The responses he got back were depressing at best.

Isaac Asimov, the famed quantum physicist, replied, "As far as I can see there is no purpose to life." Karl Jung, the Austrian psychiatrist, answered saying, "I don't know what the meaning or the purpose of life is, but it looks as if there were something meant by it." Arthur Clark, who wrote *2001: A Space Odyssey*, said, "I'm afraid I have no concrete ideas of the purpose of life." Albert Ellis, the psychiatrist who invented RET therapy, wrote back, "As far as I can tell, life has no special or intrinsic meaning or purpose." With a sense of resignation Joseph Heller responded, "I have no answers to the meaning of life and I no longer want to search for any."[8]

These are tragic statements. A life without purpose is a life not worth living. It is no accident that as our culture has turned its back on God the suicide rate has increased. In his *Reflections on the Human Condition*, philosopher Eric Hoffer spoke directly to this correlation: "We need not only a purpose in life to give meaning to our existence but also something to give meaning to our suffering."[9] When you remove God from the picture, the remaining canvas seems empty and unfulfilling, and the options for meaning and purpose become minimal. Why continue to live in the pain of purposelessness with no remedy in sight?

Suicide is the second greatest killer of teenagers in America. There is a reason for that. No one, in my estimation, says it better than the brilliant Christian apologist Ravi Zacharias, who once wrote, "We have given our children contradictory assumptions about life and then are shocked at their evil behavior and the disintegration of their lives."[10]

We cannot systematically debase a generation through distorted instructions and still expect them to have a healthy view of the worth of man. What we devalue in the classroom we destroy in the streets. As we dispose of our unwanted fetuses, we bury our young in increasing numbers. The cries of pain in the offices of the abortion clinics are muffled by the sounds of gunfire in the streets. To devalue the purpose of being is to destroy the sacredness of life.

Bertrand Russell, the renowned English mathematician and philosopher, was born into a Christian home and taught to believe in God. But he rejected his training and became an outspoken atheist. His daughter, Katherine Tait, said of him, "Somewhere at the bottom of his heart, in the depths of his soul, there was an empty space that once had been filled by God, and he never found anything else to put in it." But in spite of his spiritual blindness, he was intellectually honest when he admitted the severe consequences of rejecting the existence of God. Russell conceded, "Unless you assume a God, the question about life's purpose is meaningless."[11] What you believe determines who you are, and who you are determines what you become in life. Our destination is inseparably connected to our origin. Our purpose in life is the by-product of our inner knowledge of who we are.

Who Determines Who I Am?

When it comes to the discovery and development of your destiny, recognizing the need to separate from others is a prerequisite to understanding who you are as an individual. There is no way I could have understood and embraced my uniqueness if I had relied on others, directly or indirectly, to define my gifting, prescribe my course or discover my purpose for being. God alone has the right to define us, and He does so through the revelation of His Word. Nobody else has the right to define you.

Other qualified people can help to *refine* you, but no matter how altruistic their intentions, they cannot *define* you. Your husband cannot fully define you. Your wife cannot fully define you. Your parents cannot fully define you. Your church cannot fully define you. Society cannot fully define you. All human relationships, no matter how well meaning, are working with limited information about who you really are.

Other people's perceptions of who we are *currently* are based on our relationship to them or who we *could be* in relationship to them. Therefore, subconsciously the relationship becomes the focal point of the definition. Their inner longings and unmet needs cast a long shadow over our lives, and we find ourselves unable to grow in that place of darkness. To make matters even more frustrating, most of the time we are not even capable of fully defining ourselves. The right to define you is reserved for the One who created you.

As Myles Munroe has eloquently stated:

> You will never discover who you were meant to be if you use another person to find yourself. You will never know what you can do by using what I've done to measure your ability. You will never know why you exist if you use my existence to measure it. All you will see is what I've done or who I am. If you want to know who you are, look at God. The key to understanding life is in the source of life, not in the life itself. You are who you are because God took you out of Himself. If you want to know who you are, you must look at the Creator, not the creation.[12]

The futility of trying to understand the identity of man by asking him, "Who are you?", is graphically depicted in Romans 9 where Paul thunders out the intimidating question, "Does not the potter have power over the clay, from the same lump to make one vessel for honor and another for dishonor?"[13] The Master Potter reserves the right to mold our lives according to His divine determination for our future.

Our human tendency is to define people based on our perception of their practices. But God defines people based on His revelation of their potential. Thus, for many people, perception is the ultimate reality, even though it may not be the ultimate truth.

If you perceive yourself to be defeated, then regardless of what God says about you, your expectation produces defeat in your life. If you perceive yourself to be poor, helpless and hopeless with limited resources, talents and abilities, then it is almost as though God says, "Be it unto you according to your faith." In spite of how God sees you, in spite of His plan for you, in spite of the gifts He has given you, your faith in the negative attributes creates a world for you contrary to the plan God designed.

This principle also applies to our expectations and perceptions of others. If we perceive other people to be something other than what they are, our perception is false. And many times those people will live up—or down—to our expectations. For example, when parents perceive their children to be of little value and constantly belittle them, those children grow up with little self-worth and little confidence in their abilities.

Perception may be the ultimate reality, but it isn't always the ultimate truth!

The parable of the talents in Matthew 25 is a good example of someone living according to their false perception of God. The master gave one servant five talents, another two and another one—each according to his own ability. He knew who could handle five and who could only handle one. Then the master came back and settled accounts with them. The first and second servants doubled their talents.

Then the master asked the third servant what he did with his talent. The servant said, "I knew you to be a hard man, reaping where you have not sown, and gathering where you have not scattered seed. And I was afraid, and went and hid your talent in the ground."[14] In essence, the master said to him, "If that is how you perceive me, then that is what you are going to get back from me." The man's perception created his expectation. His expectation formed his faith. And his faith created an environment contrary to the master's plan.

What You See Is What You Get

When we do not discern ourselves or one another by the Spirit of God, we create false expectations of what we are capable of accomplishing. That is why Paul warned the Corinthian Christians to know no man after the flesh.[15] To know people after the flesh is to create false perceptions, and those false perceptions always create false expectations. Conversely, to know others by the Spirit of God is to see them in light of their potential.

Our perception always invites a response; it determines (and in some cases even creates) our reception. How do you perceive others? How do you see yourself? Some of the great heroes of faith in the Bible struggled with an inadequate perception of themselves.

- Moses appeared dreadfully inadequate with his stuttering tongue and his need for anger-management classes.

- Gideon was the poster boy for low self-esteem.

- Isaiah had a "woe is me, I am undone" complex.

- Jeremiah modeled the original "Peter Pan" syndrome: "I'm just a little boy, Lord."

- Peter was plagued with spiritual cowardliness and saw himself as a pebble instead of "The Rock."

- Paul saw himself as a religious zealot: He murdered God's children and thought he was doing God a favor!

None of these individuals saw themselves as God saw them. For example, God called Gideon a mighty man of valor, and Gideon called himself the least of his father's household. Our perception of who we are is not always in concert with God's understanding of who we are. Many times we choose—either consciously or unconsciously—to resist what God says about us and to hold to the identity of the flesh. Or we allow others to define us based upon their perception of who we are. Both are equally dangerous.

Although other people cannot define you, they can refine you. God will send people into your life, both good and bad, to refine your character. He uses others, through positive and negative relationships, to reveal and refine what is in your heart. He will use specific people to reveal the positive qualities that you need to reinforce in your life, and others to expose the negative qualities that you need to reject. Thus, friends, family, spiritual leaders and even enemies can help you refine what God has placed within you. But the revelation of your essential identity is determined by the One who formed you in His image and likeness.

It is paradoxical that the very relationships we need in order to live full, productive lives can be barriers to destiny, in that they make demands on us and often define us in a way that can mislabel who we really are. The most powerful force in the universe outside of God is human relationships. Your relationships are the key to your personal success or failure; they will either coach you into destiny or restrict you from your ultimate purpose. Everything that we are today, good and bad, is a product of the people we know and the lessons we've learned.

Let me share a couple of examples of wrong relationships. You may be attending a church to which God did not lead you. You may be working in a company that is not conducive to your spiritual health. You may be dating an unbeliever. You may be in business with someone who refuses to honor your value system. These are examples of the types of relationships that hold a potential for hindering your spiritual growth and maturity.

Wrong relationships are not always comprised of evil people. Many times good people are trapped in relationships that are simply not right...for them. I have met people who have joined a church because they were attracted to a program, a musical style or the children's ministry—not because the Father had set them there. When they finally realized they were in the wrong place, they looked for carnal reasons to justify their departure. Rather than seeking the will of God, they looked for failures in the church leadership in order to give them a reason for leaving.

> **The meaning of our existence is not invented by ourselves, but rather detected.**
>
> —*Viktor Frankl*

Relationships are complex—both have static and dynamic aspects associated with them. While certain covenant relationships are forever, those people within the relationship are in the process of growing and evolving into who they were created to be. As we become clearer on who we are individually, we must learn to communicate our discoveries to one another. Healthy relationships are vital to our inner development and our outer accomplishment even though God alone has the power to form and define us.

Origination Determines Destination

The true essence of Christianity is that of internal *being*, not external *doing*. In order to reveal the depraved condition of fallen humanity, God issued His moral directives contained in and revealed through the Ten Commandments. The Law was given to expose the individual and collective rebellion of humankind. It was not designed to empower us to become anything; it was given to teach us the knowledge of right from wrong. The focus of the Ten Commandments is on behavior modification, not identity revelation. Consequently, the Law taught us to *do* but never to *be*.

In stark contrast to the Law, Jesus came to show us who we can be through intimate union with the Father. He came to reveal the hidden destiny of fallen man.

> **Either what we do every day is important, or nothing is. In a sense we can live our entire life every day.**
>
> —*Running guru George Sheenan*

Buried beneath the layers of rejection, insecurity and misunderstanding is the person God created you to be. Destiny always begins internally and eventually manifests itself externally. It comes from the inside out—not the outside in. That's why you can put a purposeful man in an oppressive environment, and, given enough time, he will change it. But conversely, you can put a slothful man in an environment rife with potential, and he will never rise to greatness. Destiny is the result of understanding our essential identity, coming to terms with our security in the will of God and tapping into the passion for the journey.

Abraham changed the course of history because of an internal picture that was formed in his soul when he encountered the Image Maker on the backside of the desert. Moses brought deliverance to his generation because of an internal perspective that was formed when he encountered the great "I AM" in a burning bush. Joseph ruled a nation because of an internal perspective that was formed when he saw his potential in a dream. David served his generation because of an internal perspective of victory that was formed while tending his father's sheep.

Peter participated in the harvest of Pentecost because of an internal perspective that was formed when God's grace proved to be greater than his personal failures. Paul impacted the world like no other man because of an internal perspective that was formed when he was thrown from his donkey on the Damascus Road. So, as you can see, destiny always begins internally and eventually manifests itself externally. It begins with the development of an inner image of victory.

Who are you? Are you a human *being*? Or are you a human *doing*? Are you aware that the Father is pleased with you just because you are you? Or are you striving to prove something to yourself and to others? Are you struggling to do enough religious activity to drown out the condemning voices that tell you the only way to be loved by God is to work harder? That is a lie—a religious lie to keep you in bondage and hopeless futility. God's love for you isn't based on how much work you put into His kingdom. His love for you is based upon the fact that you are simply you. Unconditionally you. Uniquely you.

Seeing Into Your Destiny

1. What does it mean to be human?

2. What three characteristics are unique to the creation of man?

3. Explain the difference between the "image" and "likeness" of God as it is reflected in the creation of man.

4. Write out a three-paragraph description of yourself. Do you define yourself by who you are or what you do?

5. How healthy are the primary relationships in your life? What can you do to improve them?

Profiles in Destiny

Profiles in Destiny

When the Roman legions were withdrawn from Northern Europe in the fifth century, marauding bands of the Irish, then called Scots, began sneaking down the English coast, raiding the settlements and carrying off the spoils of battle. Among the prisoners of war was a young Englishmen named Patrick.

Although his father, who was a devout deacon of the church, raised him in a Christian home, Patrick treated his upbringing nonchalantly. But in captivity—fighting fear and loneliness—he cried out to God and was dramatically converted. As he wrote in his *Confessions*, "I would pray constantly during the daylight hours, and the love of God...surrounded me more and more."

After six years of suffering, God visited Patrick in a dream and informed him, "Thou fastest well; thou shalt soon go to thy country. Behold, thy ship is ready."

Patrick believed the Lord and began the two-hundred-mile trek to the Irish Coast where he found a ship waiting. He sailed back to the safety of England and of his family, a different young man from the one who had been taken captive.

Once again divine intervention directed the course of Patrick's future. He may have spent the rest of his life serving Christ in the safety of his native land had he not had a dream in which the babies of Ireland begged him to return to their country. He decided to return, but only after preparing himself for ministry.

The Irish of the fifth century were thoroughly entrenched in paganism. But one century after Patrick's return, Ireland became the base for the evangelization of Great Britain. The teenage prisoner turned missionary founded three hundred churches and baptized more than 120,000 people. He has come to be known as the "man who found Ireland all heathen and left it all Christian."

Chapter 6
Finding the Courage to Be

To be nobody but yourself in a world which is doing its best night and day to make you like everybody else is to fight the hardest battle any human being can fight and never stop fighting.

—E. E. Cummings

Do you have the courage to be who God created you to be? In almost two decades of pastoral counseling, I have discovered that most people fail to live life to the fullest because of fear—fear of loss, fear of poverty, fear of the unknown, fear of the future, fear of failure and even the fear of success. As a matter of fact, I probably struggle with that last fear more than any other anxiety, as do many highly driven overachievers.

I realize that it seems like a blatant contradiction—after all, why would anyone be afraid of the very thing they want most in life? And yet, strange as it may seem, some of us (or a part of all of us) are more afraid of success than failure. To succeed means that we might have to make the kind of sweeping changes that will leave us feeling displaced, insecure and vulnerable. To succeed means that we cannot retreat into the security of the comfort zone that we have carefully crafted as an excuse for failing. So we find ourselves torn between the need to succeed and the need for comfort, predictability and emotional security. As President John F. Kennedy stated, "There are risks and costs to a program of action, but they are far less than the long-range risks and costs of comfortable inaction."[1]

Our deepest fears are *always* intertwined with our greatest longings. Regardless of whether we are wrestling with the fear of poverty or the fear of aging, we long for the very thing that we fear losing or never even obtaining. Our fears serve as spiritual indicators of the deepest longings of our hearts. Aristotle explained this intrinsic connection when he proclaimed, "Courage is a mean with regard to fear and confidence."

Let me explain it this way: Most of us aren't afraid of the things that are outside the scope of possibility—the things we almost certainly never will encounter in life. For example, you probably aren't afraid of being trampled by a herd of elephants as you walk into the local shopping mall because the chance of encountering just one lone elephant is highly unlikely. It is so far outside the realm of probability that it doesn't even raise an emotional reaction.

Now contrast that strange scenario with many of the fears you actually encounter in any given week—the fear of starting a business, asking for a promotion, going back to school or trying to win a new account. I've counseled people who have divorced and are deathly afraid of getting remarried. I've ministered to others who are afraid to let go of the tightly held reins of their lives and trust God to take control. They have chosen the path of self-preservation for so long that they fear if they give up, God may make choices for them that are unpleasant. Their deepest longing is for God to lead them, but their greatest fear is *where* He might lead. Our deepest fears are always intertwined with our greatest longings.

When you fully understand this principle then you will stop rebuking your fears until you have first stopped long enough to listen to them. Sometimes we deny and even displace the fear without ever stopping to ask the question, "What is this fear trying to tell me about myself? What is it masking? What inner longing am I afraid of acknowledging in my life?" I have come to believe that although fear is evil and certainly should be driven from our lives, it should first be considered, processed and even listened to. Fear is a spiritual indicator of an unmet need or an inner longing that God desires to fill in our lives. It is an illusion pointing us to a greater reality.

Fear is a thief. It robs us of our potential and prevents us from moving forward toward our purpose in life. When we live in fear we invite the powers of failure into our lives to diminish our gifts, talents and abilities. Former NFL quarterback Fran Tarkenton once said, "Fear causes people to draw back from situations; it brings on mediocrity; it dulls creativity; it sets one up to be a loser in life." Fear is the price you must pay to move forward into the world of the unknown, untried and unexpected.[2]

Fear creates unwanted outcomes. Michael Pritchard called fear "that little darkroom where negatives are developed."[3] Fear dulls our dreams.

We dream in Technicolor.

We fear in black and white.

What Is Your Greatest Fear?

I recently watched a television documentary on the way elephants are trained. A young elephant was chained by the foot to a stake in the ground. After it tried unsuccessfully to dislodge the stake, it finally accepted the restraint and learned to stay within the circumference allowed by the length of the chain. Finally, the animal gave up its efforts to move outside of the circle. Now here is the intriguing part: As the elephant grows larger and stronger, it becomes quite capable of uprooting the stake. But because it has long since accepted that it is impossible to be free, it doesn't even try to escape. The elephant is no longer bound by a physical restraint; it is bound by an illusion. It is not limited by an outside force—it is restricted by a memory.

The world is filled with people running away from fear but making very little progress. The problem is that the illusion is masking an unmet need or an unfulfilled desire. It is over-whelming to consider the web of addictions that rule our society because we have traded the bondage of fear for the bondage of dependence. Anne Wilson Schaef analyzed our cultural psyche in her book *When Society Becomes an Addict*, and she discovered that millions of people are attempting to escape the bondage of personal fear by embracing addictions that serve as emotional anesthesia.[4]

We all have fears.

Psychologists tell us that the greatest fear shared by most Americans is the fear of public speaking. And yet man's greatest fear, universally, is the fear of death. I find that ironic. We are, as Americans, afraid of speaking while the rest of the world is afraid of dying. But September 11, 2001, changed that for us. The terrorist attack on the World Trade Center ushered in a new era of fear into the lives of most Americans by capitalizing on mankind's greatest fear—the fear of death.

When Jesus Christ embraced His destiny on the cross, He once and for all time destroyed the power of death.[5] Therefore, if Jesus is capable of overcoming the greatest fear known to man, none of our lesser fears are insurmountable to Him.

Second Timothy 1 comforts us with these words, "God has not given us a spirit of fear, but of power..."[6] This power that we have been given is not just the power to overcome—it is the power to become who we are.[7] The key to overcoming fear is to become who you are called to be in Christ.

Facing the Longing

One day several years ago, in a quiet time of prayer and meditation the Lord asked me a series of startling questions: "How would you act if you knew it was impossible to fail?" "What would you do if you were suddenly set free from every confining limitation that has been placed upon your life?" "Where would you go?" "What would you attempt?" "How would you be living?"

These questions shook me to the core of my being. Inherently I knew the answers, but I was unwilling to face them. You see, the gospel has *already* set us free from every confining limitation the world has placed upon us. To know and act upon the will of God is to experience success in life. When Jesus surrendered His life on the cross, He broke the power of sin and death, announcing to us, "You can be free to be who I created you to be. Live large. Take risks. Act in a way that is consistent with what you believe. You don't have to be afraid of the possibilities of the unknown."

I believe there is a form of righteous pretense that God just loves. There is nothing wrong in acting as if you were born to royalty. As a father, when my boys were little I enjoyed watching them swagger around the backyard acting as if they had subdued the planet. It was an outward manifestation of the inner security they had developed. Unfortunately, many Christians settle for a lesser quality of life than what God has promised and are content to live far beneath our spiritual rights and privileges.

Many of us are like the slaves who, following the Emancipation Proclamation, refused to go free because they had been deceived into believing that freedom was only a myth. That seems hard for us to imagine. Our immediate reaction is to scoff at their ignorance. *How could one choose to continue living in dehumanizing conditions and willingly choose to be treated as chattel?* we wonder. And yet we do the very same thing where our spiritual lives are concerned. We *are* free, but all too often we continue to live inside the prison cells of "self-imposed captivity." Even though the flesh, the world and the devil are unable to confine or contain us, the imagined walls within our minds say, "Don't take a risk—it could get a whole lot worse. What if you fail?" And so we withdraw, hoping that conservative living will insulate us from the possibility of failure. And we settle for merely existing in our self-imposed prison cells, settling for something less than what God has created us to be.

When the United States armed forces liberated Kabul, Afghanistan, from the control of the fundamentalist Islamic Taliban regime, a few women waited for weeks to remove the heavy *burqas* and *hijabs* that symbolized their oppression. When asked why they were waiting so long, one woman replied, "No one told me I could take it off. And what would happen if the Taliban were to ever recapture the city?" While other women danced joyously in the streets, her inner fear kept her in self-imposed captivity. She was free externally, but not internally.

> **Courage faces fear and thereby masters it. Cowardice represses it and is thereby mastered by it.**
>
> —*Martin Luther King Jr.*

The Perfect Storm

In the fall of 1991 the *Andrea Gail* left Gloucester, Massachusetts, headed for the fishing grounds of the North Atlantic Ocean. One month later an event took place that had never occurred in modern history. Hurricane Grace, moving up from the Caribbean, had all but headed out to sea when it merged with an offshore storm, creating what meteorologists described as the "perfect" storm. With howling winds of ninety miles per hour and offshore seas that towered at one hundred feet, the coastline was battered beyond recognition. The property damage was estimated at thirty-five million dollars, and the loss of life numbered six causalities—the crew of the swordfish longliner the *Andrea Gail*. The storm became the basis for Sebastian Junger's best-selling novel, *The Perfect Storm*.

In Matthew 14 the disciples were caught in the middle of an unexpected storm on the Sea of Galilee. They were afraid. "Going to sea is like going to prison, with a chance of drowning besides," wrote Samuel Johnson, the eighteenth-century English poet and essayist. Nowhere does man feel more insecure than on rough seas with little more than the deck of a boat beneath our feet to give us stability.

Battered about by the wind and the waves, the disciples fought to gain control of their fishing boat when Jesus unexpectedly arrived, walking on the water to reach them. His journey across the Sea of Galilee was a supernatural lesson in the power of the King over the material realm, which He originally created for His glory. But it is more than that. It is a picture of His promise to be with us through the uncertainties that every believer encounters.

When we understand the history behind the miracle, we see that Jesus is doing far more than simply exercising His power over the wind and waves. The water in this story is a metaphor for the challenges, hindrances and crises we face in life. Even though the Hebrews probably didn't believe in the legendary monsters of the Canaanites, they did believe in the existence of evil creatures. That's why the writers of the Old Testament used sea monsters as images of wickedness. Leviathan, the indescribable beast that rises up out of the sea, was a symbol of terror.[8] The word *rahab* was another ancient way of describing this evil crocodile...this mystical sea monster...this mysterious creature that held the power to devour and destroy.[9] Furthermore, the original Hebrew word for sea is *Yamm*, which was the name of the evil sea god in ancient Canaan myth. For the Canaanites, *Yamm* was the chaos monster. Both Psalm 89 and Job 9 speak of God ruling the raging sea, treading on the waves and stilling them.

Enter Jesus. As the disciples are shaking in terror, uncertain about the future, Jesus suddenly appears in the midst of the perfect storm. By walking on the water, He proves to them that He has been given all authority over the god of chaos, the power of the unknown. The greatest fear that rises up in the heart of man is inconsequential when lined up against the authority of Christ. By walking on the water, Jesus demonstrates the manner in which life is to be lived.

Now picture Peter. He sees Jesus dancing on the perfect storm, and in one glorious burst of revelation he understood the message behind the miracle. As a child, Peter had heard the Canaanite myths. He was familiar with the Hebrew legends. He knew the dark images of the prophetic writings. And in one unrestrained moment of inspiration Peter cried out, "Lord, if that is You out there, give me the courage to be who You have created me to be. Let me dance with You. Let me share in Your kingdom authority. Let me, as a believer; tread upon the powers of darkness."[10]

Why Peter? Why not James or John? Why not Andrew or Bartholomew? After all, Peter was the disciple with the foot-shaped mouth. I have a friend who calls him the "Joey Butaffuco of the first-century church." He was a lousy friend. He had a bad temper. He was impatient, impetuous, always in trouble and extremely unpopular at times. Why didn't Jesus invite someone a little more sophisticated, refined, charismatic, diplomatic—someone with more *joie de vivre?*

The Courage to Be Fully Human

God chose Peter because he wasn't afraid to be human. To be human means to be fallible and frail; it means to take the risk that you might not (or might) succeed. The words *human*, *humorist* and *humility* all come from the same word. To be human means to be finite. It is the opposite of God. God is infinite. We are not.[11] That simply means we are still in the process of growing and developing—we're not perfect. There are times when we will fail. That's why Jesus chose Peter, to show us that failure isn't permanent.

Several years ago I read a plaque that listed the ten rules for being human. Although the source is not known, the wisdom is readily recognized. I have adapted it to be consistent with the principles contained within the Scriptures.

1. You are a spirit being confined to a human experience until your life is over.

Created in the image of a Triune God, man is a tripartite being—spirit, soul and body. The eternal dimension of our being is the inner man, which is why someone once defined humanity as, "You *are* a spirit, you *have* a soul and you *live* in a body." We are bigger than the temporal, material challenges we face in life. Daily we walk through a symphony of pathos, frustration, turmoil, heartache and fear. We continue to grow in grace and wisdom because we are bigger than the obstacles we encounter.

2. You will receive a body. You may like it or hate it, but it will be yours for your entire time here on earth.

My children are convinced that the ability to eat chocolate chip cookies and drink ice-cold milk may be one of the greatest joys we have in life. The body each of us receives is a gift from God and is intended to be used to glorify Him. Paul taught the Ephesians that we are compelled to glorify God with our bodies because we have been purchased by the shed blood of Christ.[12] But what does it mean to glorify God in a manner worthy of His sacrifice? To listen to some Christians you would come to believe that the physical dimension of man is to be used only for religious activities: church services, prayer meetings, choir rehearsals and personal evangelism. As important as those activities are, they are not worthy enough of the life of Christ. The only thing that is worthy is you! Therefore in being yourself you glorify God.

3. You are enrolled in a full-time school called life. Study hard and learn all you can.

Each day in this school you will have the opportunity to learn important lessons. You may appreciate what you are learning or consider it irrelevant to the plans you have for the future, but every lesson will be needed to find and fulfill your destiny.

4. There are no mistakes that cannot be redeemed.

Growth is a process of trial and error; it is the result of healthy experimentation. Those experiments we consider to be "failures" are as much a part of the process as the successful experiments. The only time a person truly fails at anything is when he or she stops trying.

5. A lesson is repeated until it is learned.

A lesson will be presented to you in various forms until you have learned it. When you have learned it, you can then move on to the next lesson. There is no part of life that does not contain lessons. If you are alive there are still lessons to be learned.

6. "There" is no better than "here."

When your "there" has become a "here," you will simply obtain another "there" that will again look better than "here." The grass may appear to be greener on the other side of the fence, but sometimes that is the result of having been planted over a septic tank! Find someplace in life to put down roots. Stay planted in one place long enough, and you will bear fruit.

7. Others are merely mirrors of you.

You cannot love or hate something about another person unless it reflects something you love or hate about yourself. As painful as it may be to face, many times other people only mirror the attitudes we project toward them. That's why Jesus taught us to return good for evil. When you bless someone who spitefully uses you, you set a positive cycle in motion.[13]

8. The answers for life are all around you.

All you need to do is ask, seek, knock and have faith in God. When Moses appealed for some supernatural gift to enable him to overcome the hardened heart of Pharaoh, God asked, "What is that in your hand?"[14] An ordinary, inconspicuous, inanimate rod became the object of supernatural power. Our lives are filled with ordinary objects that can be used to the glory of God.

9. What you make of your life is up to you.

God gives each one of us all of the tools and resources we need to live the successful Christian life. What we do with them is up to us. The choice is yours. Bury your talent or steward it; you will give an account for the way you handled your relationships and resources.

10. Even though you may forget these ten rules, the reality of life is that you will also go through your life using these basic rules.

Finding Inner Congruence

Peter had the courage to be fully human. But it was Peter's temperament that also put him in danger. I've heard people say that Peter sank either because of sin in his life, doubt and unbelief in his heart or some other unresolved issue. But the truth is he began to sink, not because he was wicked, but because he was willing to be Simon Peter.

While the other disciples were safe and sound in the boat, Peter was out on the water. They didn't sink because it never occurred to them to leave the vessel. They were conservative men of prudence, reliability and common sense. They knew the difference between the land and the water. Fish swim. People walk. Water is for fish. Land is for people. But not Peter! In one glorious burst of revelation, it all came together for him. He saw the water and land converge into one magnificent opportunity to perform the impossible. So he acted on the impulse of the moment and followed the dictates of his heart, not waiting for the laggard reason. This was the glory of who he was! It was what made him Peter. It was what empowered him to do what nobody else was able to do.

But Peter's greatest strength was also his greatest weakness. Those same qualities that in the hand of Christ were used to strengthen the church sometimes brought him to the verge of ruin. It was Peter only who began to walk, and it was Peter only who began to sink. He was led into danger on these stormy waters because he consistently saw himself differently than the way in which he naturally performed. He lacked inner congruence—the harmony of mind and heart. His mind saw one thing; his heart said something different.

> The paradox of courage is that a man must be a little careless of his life in order to keep it.
>
> —*G. K. Chesterton*

Peter saw himself differently than Jesus saw him—and that worked on two levels. Peter never embraced his potential for greatness until Jesus acknowledged it in him. Conversely, he never faced his capacity for failure until Jesus acknowledged it in him. In Matthew 16, Jesus exposed Peter's lack of inner harmony by pointing out the inconsistency between his immediate identity and his ultimate destiny: "Blessed are you, Simon Bar-Jonah, for flesh and blood has not revealed this to you, but My Father who is in heaven. And I also say to you that you are Peter, and on this rock I will build My church, and the gates of Hades shall not prevail against it."[15] Although Peter saw himself as Simon—the reed, Jesus saw him as Peter—the rock.

On one occasion Jesus cautioned, "Simon, Simon! Indeed, Satan has asked for you, that he may sift you as wheat."[16] And on another He warned, "Before the rooster crows, you will deny Me three times."[17] Both times Peter denied the possibility of failure, saying, "No way! I don't believe that or receive that!" Peter lacked inner congruence. His head and his heart were not in harmony. He needed the alignment of both to come together.

Jesus does the same for us. He reveals the potential that we have never discovered lying deep within ourselves. And He also shows us that our greatest strength has the capability of also being our greatest weakness.

If you are going to be everything God has created you to be, you need inner congruence. Your head and your heart must come into alignment through the recognition of your greatest strengths and the humble acknowledgement of your greatest weaknesses. Only as you recognize both your strengths and your weaknesses is Christ able to strengthen, sustain and empower you to be who He created you to be.

Do you really know yourself? According to Jeremiah 17, the heart is dishonest above all things and cannot be fully known by personal internal analysis.[18] In other words, those around you probably see your heart better than you see it. That is why we need the mind of Christ. We don't really know who we are apart from the mind of Christ, which empowers us to see ourselves as God sees us.

Apart from God we are consigned to struggle to know and understand ourselves. In their desperate attempts to know themselves, many people immerse themselves in self-help seminars, psychotherapy and cosmic humanism. Others participate in ancient Indian rituals, seek out Eastern mystics and explore the supernatural, trying to understand who they are. However, none of these pathways bring them in touch with the revelation of their true identity, because only God is capable of defining them.

It takes the Creator to define the creation. It takes the manufacturer to tell us what components are in the product. Only the One who loves us most knows us best. Though we may gain some insight into our identity in the pivotal moments of life, we will never fully know who we are apart from the mind of Christ.

Jesus not only came to save us, but He also came to show us that He was human. He came to say, "I can do it. And because I can do it, if you will let Me help you, you can do it as well." Jesus Christ was tempted in every way that we are. He wrestled with the same issues that we wrestle with. Jesus went to the garden and said, "Lord, I don't want to give My life on the cross. Is there any way I can avoid this? It's going to be painful.

Nevertheless, if it is what You really want from Me, I'll do it. Give Me the courage to be."

The beauty of the gospel is that Jesus Christ brings us into relationship with Himself and gives us everything that He is so we can become one with Him. Only Jesus modeled true congruence—the alignment of head and heart. Even though He encountered the challenges of life and voiced His questions about God's purpose, He still had an outer conformity to His inner identity.

Perhaps you are struggling with this lack of inner congruence. The way you perceive yourself is very different from the way you really are. That is why every person needs to be saved not only from his sin but also from himself. Knowing this, God, in His desire to save us, gave us a Man—not a message, but a Man who had the courage to be fully human—exactly who He was, no more and no less. The beauty of Jesus is that He is everything He professes to be. He promises no more than He delivers and no less than He is capable of giving. He models congruence—outer conformity to His inner identity.

> **Courage is contagious. When a brave man takes a stand, the spines of others are often stiffened.**
>
> —*Billy Graham*

The Courage to Be Vulnerable

Jesus chose Peter because he was willing to be vulnerable. He was not embarrassed or ashamed to be transparent about his fear. He had fear just like the eleven in the boat, but he wasn't ashamed to hang his fear out there for everyone to see. That's vulnerability. Jesus chose Peter because Peter understood that as long as he was on Planet Earth he would always be in the process of childlike growing. And that is *true freedom*. True freedom is not being insulated from failure; true freedom is understanding that even though you are frail and are guaranteed to fail, you will grow and develop through your failures.

What was the difference between the eleven who stayed in the boat and Peter who failed? They seem to be suffering from performance anxiety. Afraid to fail, they remained behind in the security of the boat. But Peter had a grace focus. He was free from the fear of failure because he had the most incredible life jacket in the universe—a life jacket of grace. Peter understood that his ultimate purpose wasn't dependent upon his immediate performance. And when he failed, he understood that it was not his work or his performance that determined the outcome of his life—it was the work of God. It was the performance of Jesus Christ. So he could say, "Lord, save me."

Your life purpose is not dependent upon your momentary performance. That is good news. It is good news when you are doing well—and when you are not doing so well. It's good news when you succeed, because success is not always perpetual. And it is good news when you fail, because failure, as a wise man once said, "is written in pencil." If your purpose isn't contingent upon your performance, then when you perform well, God is in control. And when you perform badly, God is still in control. Your purpose was established from before the beginnings of the earth, and it is not based upon how well you perform at everything you attempt.

This principle is true of believers individually and corporately as the church. Every church is bound to have some great services where the anointing seems to be so thick it oozes through our lives. But those incredible moments are usually followed by services so dry we wonder if were hallucinating. Thank God our purpose is not contingent upon our performance. I've found that "success" is a matter of averaging out the "highs" and "lows" and living off your *purpose*—not your *performance*. We all go through those moments in life when we are elevated and celebrated, as well as those when we are tolerated and acknowledged. That's life! But in reality, our purpose is greater than celebration or toleration. Our purpose is dependent upon the One who established it—the One who said, "I know what I have begun in you. And what I have begun, I will complete."[19]

The Courage to Risk

Despite the humanistic overtones, Soren Kierkegaard's statement does ring true: "It requires courage not to surrender oneself to the ingenious or compassionate counsels of despair that would induce a man to eliminate himself from the ranks of the living; but it does not follow from this that every huckster who is fattened and nourished in self-confidence has more courage than the man who yielded to despair."[20]

Peter had the courage to take a risk; he knew he could step out and maybe succeed, or step out and possibly fail. Either way, he had a life jacket called *grace*, which would sustain him in the midst of the raging storms of life.

God chooses people who stumble and fall; the Bible is filled with their stories. Look at King David. Not only did he commit adultery, but he also committed murder—and God still chose him. Samson's adult life was geared toward three promises that he made to God. He broke every one of them—and God still chose him. Judas has become a synonym for failure. He was one of the twelve disciples, yet he committed suicide. Judas couldn't deal with failure.

The difference between Judas and Peter is that Judas allowed his failure to become permanent. Judas did not say, "Lord, save me," as Peter did. Judas's sin was no worse than Peter's, for Peter also denied and betrayed Christ. But Judas couldn't deal with failure. He condemned himself. He didn't realize that his success was not based upon performance. Peter shattered his vows, and yet God chose him in advance knowing that he would. God knew that in his weakness, Peter would cry out.

Sin is not about failing. Sin is about refusing to say, "Lord, save me." Sin is not about the mistakes we make. Sin is about whether we turn to the grace of God in the midst of the mistake or allow self-condemnation to reinforce our alienation from the grace of God.

The root of sin keeps us from the presence of God—that is New Testament theology. That is why Jesus didn't come with a list of rules, even though He intended to fulfill the holiness and righteousness of the Old Testament. Jesus came as a man to show us the beauty of a life dependent upon the Father. He shows us that sin in the New Testament is about being separated from our source. It is not about a litany of all the wrong things we do in life. The sin we encounter in life is when we turn our back on the grace of God. We must be like Peter and turn to God in the midst of our fear.

Fear can be either a steppingstone to deliverance and greatness or a spiritually debilitating experience that will keep us from living life to the fullest. Sin always limits the quality of our human experience.

Remember the parable we examined briefly in the previous chapter about the owner of an estate who had three servants? Matthew 25 records the parable of the master who went away, leaving his servants behind. In preparation for his departure he gave one servant five talents, another two talents and the final servant one talent. He told them, "Do something with it." He went away, and when he came back, he asked the first servant, "What did you do?"

The servant said, "I had a great stock tip. You know, the market was really up. I invested it and doubled your money."

He asked the second servant what he did, and he said, "Well, I had a great opportunity. I opened up a little coffee shop, and called it 'Starducks.' (Forgive the pun; I just couldn't resist.) I put it down on the corner of the marketplace. And I doubled what you entrusted to me."

The master asked the third servant what he did, and the servant said, "I just want to get through life without too much damage, so I took what you gave me and I buried it."

The master asked, "Why?"

"Because I was afraid," the servant replied.

Think about that for a moment. It wasn't that he lacked opportunity or because the economy was bad or even because the risk was too great. He lived a conservative life because of fear. Then the master said, "Take what I gave you and give it to the first servant," and he cast out the unprofitable servant.[21]

Fear is debilitating. Fear is limiting. It kills relationships. It destroys churches. It aborts destinies. It decimates businesses. Fear will keep us from being who God created us to be. When we play it safe because of fear, we have the tendency to withdraw and be conservative. "If I love, I may be hurt. If I give, I may not get back. If I risk, I might fail. I don't know what is out there. Maybe what I have settled for is better than how bad it could be." Conservative living creates wasted opportunities. Jesus calls us to risk.

> **Risk! Risk anything! Care no more for the opinion of others, for those voices. Do the hardest thing on earth for you. Act for yourself. Face the truth.**
>
> —*Katherine Mansfield*

Jesus chose Peter not only because he was willing to fail, but also because he was willing to risk his life to Jesus. Peter was willing to risk it all when he stepped out of the boat to walk on the water to Jesus. And what happened? Peter had an incredible experience—he was actually walking on water! I find that astonishing! How many people in the history of the world can actually claim that? It must have been exhilarating. His obedience to Jesus was paying off in a way he dared never imagine. But then Peter began to sink; his faith was tested in new ways—and it was frightening. But in spite of his fear, in spite of the cold water splashing all around him and the weight of his clothing trying to drag him under, he maintained enough presence of mind to cry out, "Lord, save me!" His fear did not invalidate his faith. Instantly, Jesus stretched out His hand to Peter and caught him. And once more Peter was on top of the water. He probably looked at Jesus and said, "Wow! This is incredible!" I suspect that Jesus just smiled.

What happened next is remarkable—but it's also easy to miss. The Scripture says, *"And when they got into the boat..."* Think about that. They were some distance from the boat when Peter began to sink. How did he get back to the boat? There are two options. Either Jesus picked him up, threw him over his shoulder and carried him to the boat, or, after one touch from the Master, Peter rose back up in faith and walked with Jesus back to the boat.

Picture the scene. Jesus and Peter walk back across the waves—the wind is still boisterous, the waves are still crashing, the eleven disciples are still cowering—nothing has changed. But note this—when they got into the boat, the wind ceased. This implies that Peter had to walk back across that stormy body of water. Jesus didn't say, "Once I have settled the storm you will have the courage to get home." He simply said, "Come on, Peter. Let's face this storm together." And together they walked across the stormy sea until together they climbed into the boat. Then Jesus said, "All right; now that you have experienced victory, let Me show you what else I can do here. Wind, be still!"

Jesus gave Peter a second chance to be Peter. He gave him the opportunity to bring heart and head into alignment. He gave Peter the courage to be.

Do you have the courage to be who He created you to be?

Seeing Into Your Destiny

1. Do you have the courage to find out what your life could really be?

2. How are your deepest fears and greatest longings intertwined?

3. How would you act if you knew it was impossible to fail?

4. What do you think about the ten rules for being human? What can be learned by these rules? What dangers must be avoided?

5. Write one paragraph describing your greatest strength. How could it also become your greatest weakness?

Profiles in Destiny

Profiles in Destiny.

In the year 1870 the United Brethern churches in Indiana held their annual conference. As the president of the college where they were meeting addressed the group, he told them they were living in an exciting time of great invention and that he believed, for example, that man would someday fly through the air like birds.

The presiding bishop didn't think much of this statement. As a matter of fact, he called it heresy, saying that the Bible taught that flight was reserved for the angels— not for mere mortal man. His comments killed the meeting's excitement.

When the bishop returned home, he told his family what the president of the college had said and how ridiculous it was. But although his words had destroyed the ability of his listeners at the convention to dream of a day when men flew like the birds, his two young sons, Wilbur and Orville, looked at things a little differently than old dad. They had a "higher" perspective than their father, Bishop Milton Wright. They possessed a dream—and it could not be taken from them by mere words. And of course you already know the rest of the story—the Wright brothers invented the first flying machine. I wonder if the Wright brothers would have invented the airplane if they had not had a vision planted in their heads by one not-so-visionary father.

Chapter 7

Born to Rule—
Trained to Reign

People are training for success when they should be training for failure. Failure is far more common than success; poverty is more prevalent than wealth; and disappointment more normal than arrival.

——J. Wallace
Hamilton

Every individual who finds and fulfills his or her destiny has to endure the process by which we mature from promise to purpose. As the old proverb goes, "The only people who start at the top are well diggers and gravediggers—and gravediggers hit bottom in about six feet." In every other field of endeavor you start at the bottom and, through faith and endurance, work your way to the top. Life is a workshop, designed with challenges and opportunities to prepare us to rule and reign throughout eternity.

Life in the kingdom of God begins with the revelation of sonship. Through faith in Jesus Christ we are made sons of God and heirs according to the promise.[1] However, our sonship alone does not qualify us to receive our full inheritance in the kingdom of God. It will position us for eternity but not necessarily for destiny. Paul described this tension in these words, "As many as are *led* by the Spirit of God, these are *sons* of God."[2] The word translated as "sons" is the Greek word *huios,* which literally means, "the *fully matured* sons" of God. The promise of our inheritance is reserved for those who are fully mature. The immature, the rebellious and the spiritually ignorant must continue the training process until they are made ready to receive their inheritance in Christ.

We must endure the process that positions us for the promise of our inheritance. Our birth into the kingdom as sons is only our entrance into kingdom life—not our final destination. Jesus said, "I am the door," not "I am the destination."[3] *The door into what?* you may wonder. He is the entrance into eternal life, spiritual sonship and the promise of our inheritance. A new world of possibility, opportunity and divine destiny awaits us beyond the door called *Christ.* Each of us is still in "process" until we learn to apply the Word of God to our lives and conform our manner of living to the scriptural pattern.

Maturity Matters

The poet Robert Browning wrote, "Why stay we on the earth except to grow?" That question should be applied to our relationship with Jesus Christ. Why are we Christians except to grow? Why does maturity matter?

The foremost reason we have been called to grow spiritually is because it brings us into position to receive everything God has promised to us in our inheritance. The Father has programmed, planned and preordained an inheritance for His people. But the inheritance is held in reserve for us until we grow up. Many believers are not receiving all that has been promised to them because they are unaware of the need to be trained until they reach maturity.

Some things in both the natural and the spiritual realms are reserved for the mature. For example, no one would put a child at the controls of powerful earth-moving equipment. Likewise, in the spiritual realm, God has ordained for believers to operate the powerful earth-moving equipment of the Holy Spirit to change the world, destroy the works of darkness and advance the purpose of His kingdom. But He will not release those who are rebellious or immature into that influential place of leadership. The Russian novelist Leo Tolstoy once said, "Everyone thinks of changing the world, but no one thinks of changing himself." Growth only comes through the willingness to change and be changed.

> In the history of the world, there have never been enough mature people in the right place at the same time.

—Anonymous

Even though we are destined to inherit all things in Christ, until the time of our maturity we are kept under "tutors" and our inheritance is kept "in trust." Our inheritance is gradually released to us as we prove our ability to properly steward it. Here's how the New International Version phrases it: "As long as the heir is a child, he is no different from a slave, although he owns the whole estate. He is subject to guardians and trustees until the time set by his father."[4] God is committed to equipping and empowering us so that when we come into our inheritance, we will be effective in what we set our hands to do. We are not released to fully possess our inheritance until we have gone through the training preparation. This principle becomes clearer as we compare the process of biblical inheritance to the modern means of acquiring wealth through get-rich quick schemes, such as the lottery.

While winning the lottery promises great gain, we've all heard the stories of people who lost everything they won and whose lives were destroyed because they were not prepared for the impact of possessing extreme wealth. They were not mature enough to handle the responsibility of the gain they received. They lacked the training necessary to maintain and expand their increase.

Receiving Your Inheritance

There are three primary words translated as "inheritance" in the Scriptures, two from the Old Testament and one from the New Testament.

The first Hebrew word is transliterated *nachalah*, which means "to occupy, to distribute, to instate or to divide so as to have." The idea being communicated through this word is that something must be defined and divided in order for it to be inherited. An example of this type of inheritance is found in Numbers 34 where the Lord commanded Moses to instruct the children of Israel: "When you come into the land of Canaan, this is the land that shall fall to you as an inheritance—the land of Canaan to its boundaries."[5] It was time for Israel to define, determine and divide the land that had become their inheritance. This was their destiny.

The second word is somewhat different from the first. The Hebrew word transliterated as *nachal* means "to take possession, to acquire, occupy by driving out, to expel." Picture what you might do to an intruder who unlawfully moved into your home, deliberately set up housekeeping and defiantly refused to move out. In a fit of righteous indignation you would *nachal* the illegal squatter. Numbers 33 reveals this very picture—but in a nation, not in a home. The Lord instructed Moses to drive out the inhabitants of the land: "Dispossess the inhabitants of the land...and you shall divide the land by lot as an inheritance among your families."[6]

There is a significant difference between these two Old Testament words. The first focuses our attention on what is to be inherited, while the other centers on the one who is to inherit and how he must prepare for and possess the inheritance. Interestingly, we have now come back to the intersection between the sovereignty of God and the responsibility of man that I described in chapter three. There are some things we receive by grace, while other things must be possessed in faith. How do you know the difference between the two? By being led by the Spirit of God. By the witness of the Holy Spirit, the fully matured son knows intuitively…instinctively…internally… when to fight and when to stand still and see the salvation of the Lord.[7]

Let's take a look at the New Testament concept of inheritance. The Greek word is transliterated as *kleronomia*, which means literally, "to break into bits." When connected with the word *law*, it takes on a different meaning: "to receive that which is broken up and parceled out." A prime example of this is found in Ephesians 1. The apostle Paul prayed for the church at Ephesus to be awakened from sleepwalking in order to discover the riches of the glory of Christ's inheritance in the saints.[8] Each of us has been given a magnificent portion of the glorious inheritance that Christ has invested in the saints. Now, we must have a revelation of our portion in order to receive everything that Christ has allotted for us.

God has willed you an inheritance in Christ, and He wants you to comprehend the scope of that inheritance. He wants to teach you His ways, give you His wisdom and make you skillful so that your work in the kingdom of God bears fruit and endures.

We're spending our children's inheritance.

—Bumper sticker on motor home

Here's the wonderful thing about the kingdom. You don't have to die to get your inheritance—it's available now, in this world. Religion teaches you just to serve Jesus miserably all through life, and when you die you go to heaven and receive a double portion for all of your pain and suffering. That attitude negates the abundant life Jesus promised. It promotes a lethargy that says, "I'm just enduring to the end so I can go and be with Jesus and have my little cabin in the sky." People with that perspective never think about being trained to reign, because they believe reigning is relegated to the millennium or to heaven. But we are called to reign in life. We make progress in the kingdom of God as faith and trust in God increase and we allow Him to lead and guide us into the things He has prepared for us.

Those who are led by the Holy Spirit are positioned by God to become mature and to qualify for their inheritance. Every believer has a powerful inheritance in the kingdom of God. But the Father releases our inheritance progressively as we mature. In both the Old and New Testament culture, it took a fully matured son to receive, earn or win in battle the inheritance he was promised.

Who Wants to Be an Inheritor?

One of the most popular television programs of the early twenty-first century is the game show *Who Wants to Be a Millionaire?*, hosted by the ubiquitous Regis Philbin. The objective is clarified in the name of the game. To play the game is to acknowledge that you want to be rich. By the way, a word of advice to those considering trying out for the game show—don't sign up if you want to live in poverty, because you just might win, and that would spoil your plan! Likewise, to become a son of God is to become a joint heir with Christ. Don't sign up if you aren't interested in finding and fulfilling your destiny. This game is real, the stakes are eternal and the reward is your inheritance—on both sides of the grave.

So what is your inheritance? Besides those things you might inherit from your natural parents, what else are you entitled to receive? Can you define it? Have you defined it? If you can't, then how are you going to position yourself to receive it?

Another way of looking at this issue is to consider what God has called you to be or to do. There comes a point in time when you must identify it, clarify it, describe it and take action toward possessing it. I often hear people say, "Well, uhh...my inheritance is to...uhhh...well...I dunno...but I think I'm getting close!" And then they waste the next twenty years of their lives on irrelevant jobs, insignificant projects and unimportant issues.

When they reach retirement age they stop long enough to look back and see what God intended for them to become. Wasted moments create wasted lives.

> **Men heap together the mistakes of their lives and create a monster, which they call destiny.**

> *—John Hobbes*

Many times we fail to clarify our objectives in life simply because it doesn't sound very *spiritual* to do so. We have been taught, falsely, that it's more spiritual to live without hopes, dreams and ambitions. "After all," the religious pundits say, "look at Jesus; He only engaged in spiritual work and never had any earthly ambitions. He is our pattern." If that is your philosophy, you are wrong on the first point and right on the second one. Jesus had a mission in life, and He is our pattern!

Jesus spent 90 percent of His life working in a carpenter's shop and 10 percent preaching, teaching and healing. For thirty years He labored at His craft and was undoubtedly very good at what He did. For those who might find that hard to believe, can you imagine Jesus doing shoddy work? There can be no doubt but that He was a tribute to His father, Joseph, and His craft. And just as He excelled in the carpenter's shop, He also fully committed to His destiny as the "Lamb slain from the foundation of the world."[9] He began with the mission in mind, and every day of His life was measured against His earthly objective.

God hasn't called you to die on His behalf, but He has called you to live and to glorify Him though the talents, gifts and anointing He invested in your life. From the moment you finish reading this book, you need to know what you want to do with the rest of your life. That may sound extremely ambitious, but it can be done if you are willing to take action. You don't have to work out all of the details of the journey before you can decide exactly that to which you want to dedicate your life. Don't be afraid to clarify the big picture. God will adjust it as you continue the journey anyway.

The Incentive for Spiritual Growth

Rather than the inheritance coming all at once, it comes to us progressively, proportionate to our spiritual growth in Christ. Thus our incentive to submit to the process of spiritual development is to receive the fullness of our inheritance. That is the most powerful incentive I can imagine. Here are just a few of the things that God wants to give you as a portion of your inheritance in Christ.

- Our inheritance is the destiny that God has chosen for us to fulfill and enjoy.[10]

- Our inheritance is the special ability with which we have been entrusted.[11]

- Our inheritance is the resource we need to accomplish the purpose of God in our lives.[12]

- Our inheritance is the wisdom to be effective in our generation.[13]

- Our inheritance is the power to defeat our enemies and walk in absolute victory.[14]

- Our inheritance is the children we have been chosen to instruct.[15]

- Our inheritance is spiritual, emotional and financial prosperity.[16]

- Our inheritance is favor with all men.[17]

- Our inheritance is rest from all our enemies.[18]

- Our inheritance is the earth.[19]

Training for Reigning

In the eleventh century, King Henry III of Bavaria grew tired of court life and the pressures of being a monarch. He made application to Pryor Richard at a local monastery, asking to be accepted as a contemplative and to spend the rest of his life in the monastery. "Your Majesty," said Pryor Richard, "do you understand that the pledge here is one of obedience? That will be hard because you have been a king."

"I understand," said Henry. "The rest of my life I will be obedient to you, as Christ leads you."

"Then I will tell you what to do," said Pryor Richard. "Go back to your throne and serve faithfully in the place where God has put you." When King Henry died, a statement was written: "The king learned to rule by being obedient."

> **Be not afraid of greatness: some are born great, some achieve greatness, and some have greatness thrust upon them.**

—William Shakespeare

Nothing in the kingdom of God is born fully matured. Everything begins as a seed, and only through the process of spiritual growth does it come to full maturity. You were born to rule, but you must be trained to reign. Your destiny is divinely deposited within you in seed form, and through faithfulness it becomes fully matured. In those times when we tire of our roles and responsibilities, it helps to remember that God has planted us in a certain place and called us to be a good steward of the realm of responsibility entrusted to us. Christ expects us to be faithful where he puts us. We will give account for our lives.

The Bible is filled with the stories of men and women who were born to rule; yet, they needed to be trained to reign. Let's look at this principle in three different people: Adam, Joseph and Jesus.

Adam Was Trained to Reign

Adam was born to rule. Everything in him was hard-wired to conquer, to dominate and to govern. He was spiritually, physically, emotionally and relationally formed to manage the planet on God's behalf. Adam had none of the limitations with which we struggle. He was formed in the image of God and filled with the life of God. He had no genetic flaws. His brain was uncontaminated from negative thinking. His identity was undeniable. His purpose was absolutely clear. Adam was a man formed in the image of God, with the responsibility and the privilege of imaging God to the rest of the world.[20]

Yet even though Adam was born to rule, even though he had unlimited ability, he still had to be trained to reign. God created this uncontaminated man without limits or hindrances, put him in the Garden of Eden and instructed him to tend it and keep it. God told Adam he could freely eat of every tree of the garden except the tree of the knowledge of good and evil. He was created to rule, but he needed to be trained to reign. Adam's training involved obedience—and so will ours.

Joseph Was Trained to Reign

Joseph was born to privilege, power and prestige.[21] Joseph knew that he was a gift from God to the world. He had heard the stories about his mother interceding to bring a son into the earth. His father proudly presented him as the treasured son that the others should honor and respect. Not only did he have his father's favor, but he also had the divine promise of greatness through God-given dreams that revealed his destiny had to do with ruling over others—his family and more.

However, just as any teenager who thinks he knows it all, Joseph's perspective of his destiny was restricted by the undisciplined view of his limited experience. Joseph's idea of how the purpose of the Lord would be fulfilled in his life was far smaller than God's intention for him. Joseph thought of ruling his family—God thought of him saving a nation from extinction.

God thought of him bringing life to his family by sheltering them safe from famine under the covering of Egypt. So God began to take Joseph through the training process. Though he was born to rule, he had to be trained to reign. Only God was able to develop the promise within Joseph into the character necessary for a kingdom-sized call.

Joseph had to submit himself to trust God, as God used the evil jealousy of his brothers to put him into the pit and sell him into slavery. He went from the pit to Potiphar's house, from Potiphar's house into prison and from the prison to being prime minister of Egypt. Through that training process, Joseph lost his arrogance and his small perspective as God used the evil intentions of others to promote good in his life. God didn't cause the evil to happen. He allowed it and used it. And God brought Joseph into a place of greater effectiveness than he could have ever dreamed of.

We see the changes in Joseph's attitude after he has been through the training process. When Joseph revealed his identity to his brothers, he told them, "I am Joseph your brother, whom you sold into Egypt. But now, do not therefore be grieved or angry with yourselves because you sold me here; for God sent me before you to preserve life."[22] Joseph was no longer angry or bitter. He didn't blame his brothers. He saw the hand of God at work. He told them, "God sent me before you to preserve you as a remnant in the earth and to keep you alive by a great deliverance. It was not you who sent me here, but God; and He has made me a father to Pharaoh, lord of all his household and a ruler over the land of Egypt." Joseph went *from* being born to rule, *through* the process of being trained to reign and *to* his God-ordained destiny of ruling and reigning under the power of God.

Jesus Was Trained to Reign

One would think that Jesus would not need to undergo training. Yet, it was no different for Jesus than for any of us. Jesus was born to rule, but He still had to be trained to reign.[23]

Imagine how difficult it must have been for Jesus. We find it difficult to learn from people who aren't as smart or as spiritual as we are—or think we are. We have this little religious way of thinking, *Well, I'm just so much more spiritually advanced than they are...how could they possibly teach me anything?* I've spoken to dozens of people throughout the course of my ministry who left churches because they were—in their own religious opinion—*so far advanced beyond the leaders at their former church.*

Imagine what it must have been like for Christ to be born into a world that He had created with His very own Word, and then be forced to learn from the very man He had created. The Creator became a servant to the created. The Sinless One became subservient to sinful men. The Perfect One was forced to learn from imperfect men. The One who had created the tree was required to learn carpentry from a mere mortal! And He did so with humility and grace. He went through the process of humbling Himself and becoming obedient, even to His death on the cross.

Jesus demonstrated the manner in which life is to be lived. Human nature says, "Don't humble yourself."

The flesh life says, "You are so much better and so much greater than this."

But the Lord says, "I want to put you in a place where you intentionally humble yourself so that I can build up the greatness I have already put inside you." If almighty God humbled Himself, how much more should we humble ourselves, learning obedience through the things that we are taught?

When Do We Start Reigning?

Romans 5 speaks of reigning in life *now* at this present time—not in heaven.[24] To reign in life means to govern the effects of life around us and to be in control of events by fulfilling the program of the Father and moving in the direction God determines. We are not waiting to rule and reign with Christ *after*

He returns in the flesh. He wants us to be delegated stewards working with Him to dominate powers of darkness and advance the kingdom of God at this moment in history. Jesus invites us to cast our care on Him, to take His yoke and learn of Him.[25] When we yoke up with Jesus Christ, we learn His ways and begin to partner with Him, ruling and reigning in this life.

In one of His more radical statements to His disciples, Jesus boldly declared that many are called, but few are chosen.[26] Let me paraphrase that: Many are invited to participate in the discovery and in the development of their destiny, but they choose not to do so. This rejection is usually based upon a misunderstanding of what is involved in the developmental process of training for reigning. Many are called, but few acknowledge the responsibility to be trained to reign. We have to move from calling to choosing, from promise to purpose, from sonship to rulership and from training to reigning.

Decision is a risk rooted in the courage of being free.

—*Paul Tillich*

Some people think that preparation time is wasted time. They think, *I'm gifted, talented and anointed. What's the holdup here? Why doesn't the leadership team see just how wonderful I really am? Why am I still doing this carpentry work? Don't they see that if I don't get started now, I might only have three and a half years of ministry? And what can you do in that little time?*

Preparation is never wasted; in fact, the journey is as important as the destination in God's eyes. During preparation time, our gifts, talents and character are refined so that they will glorify God in the manner He wants to be glorified. And there is a difference, many times, in the way we want to glorify Him and the way He wants to be glorified. We give Him sacrifice when He simply wants obedience. We try to impress Him with our talent when He wants to see the fruit of our character.

Let's Begin the Process

How do we go from calling to choosing? How do we go from promise to purpose? How do we move from sonship to ruler-ship? Here are ten life lessons to help us understand and coop-erate with the process:

Life Lesson 1. Prepare to be humbled—and possibly even humiliated.

If you have ever worked in a garden you have encountered the black-brown substance called *humus*. The word comes straight from the Latin without changes in spelling, and it means "earth." In keeping with the origin of the word, *humility* means "on the ground." The expression of true humility is born in the person who has willingly condescended from a position of pride to lay prostrate on the ground in a place of submission to almighty God.

Before we begin the process of refining our character and releasing our quality, we have to present ourselves before the Lord. We must say, "Lord, even though I see myself as this wonderfully talented individual, ready to change the world in the morning, I know that You have a better plan to get me there than the plan that I would naturally take. So whatever You need to do, Lord, in order to position me for greatness, I am hum-bling myself in order to be trained for kingdom service." That's a prayer God will rush to answer.

Brokenness is the prerequisite to usefulness in the kingdom of God. As Dr. Alan Nelson points out in *Embracing Brokenness*, "The human soul is much like an untamed stallion with his unbridled energy. Sometimes it is majestic and powerful, and at other times it is stubborn and destructively dangerous. Regardless of its potential, the untamed soul has limited capacity for constructive use. Just as the unbroken horse cannot be ridden for enjoyment or used to herd cattle, a person's unbroken spirit is confined to the sheer beauty of its potential productivity. An unbroken soul restricts God's work in a person's life."[27]

Life Lesson 2. Surrender long before you are dominated.

You will either fall on the rock and allow yourself to be broken, or the rock will fall on you, thereby crushing you.[28] Jesus taught us to pray *Thy* kingdom come, not *my* kingdom come.[29] I have a friend who often says, "The only choice we really face in life is to 'kiss the Son' or 'bite the dust.'" We must be willing to do whatever God requires of us. It is not our kingdom—it is His. The surrendering of our lives will bring greater fulfillment than if we selfishly hang on to our small perspective and our limited experience. For when we surrender our lives and rediscover our place in Christ, we are given the opportunity to see the kingdom of God expanded in the earth.

Life Lesson 3. Open your mind to new possibilities.

The Greek philosopher Plutarch wrote, "As bees extract honey from thyme, the strongest and driest of herbs, so sensible men often get advantage and profit from the most awkward circumstances." There is nothing wrong with being a kingdom opportunist. When kingdom opportunists encounter hardships, they look for the opportunities to grow, mature and advance to the next level of living. Opportunity exists where you open your eyes to look for it. Romans 12 instructs us not to be conformed to this world, but to be transformed by the renewing of our minds, that we may prove what is the good, acceptable and perfect will of God.[30] Renewing your mind is little more than training your brain to look at life differently—the way that God looks at it.

Life Lesson 4. Learn to appreciate and celebrate who you are in Christ.

As we saw in an earlier chapter, your identity is your destiny. Don't be afraid to appreciate and celebrate who you are. Don't adopt the discontented spirit that prevails in our culture and produces so much striving. Long ago I discovered that nothing is really ever *achieved* by striving—it's all *received* by grace. And nothing positions us to receive any better than an attitude of gratitude. When we appreciate and celebrate who we are, we release ourselves to grow and mature.

Life Lesson 5. Don't be afraid to esteem others above yourself.

What you make happen for others, God will make happen for you.[31] This one principle is the driving force behind this upside-down realm called *the kingdom of God*. In a world where personal agendas are fulfilled at the expense of integrity, morality and selflessness, the principles of the kingdom of God run contrary to popular opinion. Humanistic thinking seems to dictate the actions of the day. We have been led to believe that you cannot reign in life if you are serving someone else's purpose. If you lay down your agenda, how is God going to do what He has promised to do in your life? A husband may think, *If I serve my wife, how will my needs be met?* And a wife may think, *If I serve my husband, how will my personal needs be met?* Yet God designed this plan: As we serve one another, and as we serve His people, He pours into us everything that we personally have need of. He pours this sufficiency into us by His Spirit—and through those relationships.

Life Lesson 6. Transition is here to stay.

The inescapable reality of life in the twenty-first century is this: Change, or you will be changed. If there is anything we've learned from the experiences of the past few years of "doing life," it's that the near future holds anything but the expected. Gone are the days of predictability and routine. Those frameworks that have held firm for generations, providing the basic structure of life, have begun to falter. The concepts that have governed business, science, government and philosophy no longer seem to apply. The traditional formulas for interpersonal relationships cannot even guarantee the same results they once did.

For years I lived with the idea that we were simply in a "season" of change, only to wake up one day and realize that this "season" was unending. Transition is not simply a period of time in our lives—it is the whole of life. In fact, transition is the lifestyle of Spirit-led men and women. (It's vital that you distinguish between these two perspectives, because if you perceive transition to be a "momentary affliction," you will be incredibly disappointed when you move from one period of transition headlong into the next.)

A wise man once said, "All people consider change as loss, so they react adversely in the face of losing what was once constant in their lives." Is that ever true! Anyone ever involved in leading anything has encountered that attitude. As leaders in the church, we learn to handle those who fear getting lost in the crowd and losing importance as the church grows. As parents, we learn to handle our children during times of promotion, demotion and relocation. And as husbands or wives, we wonder about our own significance when our spouse succeeds in his or her respective career or ministry. We often resent change because of our fear of the unknown. Rather than seeing the possibilities inherent in this process called transition, we are intimidated by the cost associated with change. Unfortunately, we fail to realize that when we resist change we are changed by the nature of our resistance. To resist transition is to resist life.

Life Lesson 7. Determine to keep going when everyone else is exhausted.

Whether we are on the same slow pathway as Joseph (seventeen years from the pit to the palace), on the progressive track like David (thirteen years from the first anointing to the second anointing when he was named king) or on the speedway like Paul (three days from conversion to empowerment), it takes perseverance to reach the final destination. It takes determination to develop the character to rule. That is why the writer of Hebrews tells us not to become sluggish, but to imitate those who through faith and endurance inherit the promises.[32]

If you have a word from God, a dream, a vision, a prophecy or a promise that is not yet manifested in your life, I encourage you to persevere. God is faithful. If you will continue to allow Him to develop in you the character He desires, then you will discover the plan and the fulfillment of the promise in your life. In this race called *life* there is no finish line. The finish line is heaven! In the words of Yogi Berra, "It ain't over till it's over!"

Life Lesson 8. Set measurable goals, monitor them and adjust them when necessary.

When the renowned Spanish conductor Pablo Casals was in the final years of his life, a young reporter challenged him with a question: "Mr. Casals, you are ninety-five years old and the greatest cellist that ever lived. Why do you still practice six hours a day?"

What was Casal's answer? "Because I think I'm making progress." That is the type of commitment to continual growth that you should have.

I have attended a number of motivational seminars, listened to dozens of cassette tapes on building a successful career and read scores of books on motivation, time management and career planning. The one constant factor in every seminar, cassette tape and biography is the presence of goal setting. If you don't set measurable goals by which you can judge your progress (or lack thereof), you can never be sure that you are progressing through the training process. You only reach the goals you set. That's why the prophet Habakkuk instructs us to write the vision and make it plain so that he may run who reads it.[33] Through searching the mind of Christ in prayer and Bible study we are able to discern His will and set goals in accordance with His value system for our lives. Once we've clarified the objective, we ask Him to empower us and then confidently move toward it.

Don't be afraid to dream big. As you read the Bible you find that God never rebuked anyone for believing too big, asking for too much or trying too hard. He did, however, consistently chastise those of little faith who failed to ask for enough. Set your goals so high that you cannot perform them in your own strength. That will keep you dependent upon God.

Life Lesson 9. Get moving, Hero; you don't have all day.

Remember Mel Fisher, who spent fourteen years searching for a sunken Spanish galleon off the Florida Keys? Every day the diving crew went out in search of this elusive ship. Many wondered if they would ever find it or if the ship was even there. Mel had a motto that kept the crew inspired: *"Today's the Day!"* He had T-shirts made for the entire crew bearing the maxim. Then one day after fourteen long years with nothing to show for them, today *was* the day. They finally found the sunken treasure containing millions of dollars in gold and jewels. Mel Fisher's perseverance paid off.

Mel Fisher's maxim was lifted straight from the pages of Hebrews 3, where God repeatedly warns us not to postpone to tomorrow what He intends for us to do today. When presented with the promise of entering God's rest, Israel failed to respond aggressively in faith. As a result the people were sentenced to forty years of wandering in the wilderness until a new generation of faith arose.

Napoleon Hill once said, "It's not what you are going to do, but it's what you are doing now that counts." Many unsuccessful people have planed for the future but have failed to act upon the present. Planning without action is time wasted. When you take action, you won't be disappointed, even if the plan fails.

Life Lesson 10. Drop the long face; it's all right to enjoy the journey.

Life is an exciting journey, filled with exciting discoveries and rich, fulfilling moments. If you continue on this transitional journey—the journey of personal development—you have to be committed to the end result. Purpose in your heart that nothing short of God's very best is an acceptable substitute. Being grateful for the journey and for what God is accomplishing in our lives opens the door for Him to do the work He has promised—which is to release us to reign in life.

There is something about being grateful in knowing that God has us by the hand and is with us in the process. He does not withhold His goodness as we go through the process. But He empowers us and gives us what we need now so that we can make it to the full release of His purpose in our lives. Not only do we have hope for the future, but we are filled with joy as we journey toward that future. We are not waiting until every promise comes to pass before we smile. We are not waiting until all the fields in our lives are in simultaneous harvest before we praise Him. But we will live grateful and thankful lives as sons and daughters of God who are under discipline and who are good stewards in the kingdom of God.

Yes, the training process can be painful and even frustrating at times, but the grace of God will lead us through the process, empower us to endure and ultimately produce in us the final result we have been promised. Destiny will be achieved as you receive the grace of God, allow Him to be God and cooperate with Him along the pathway. You can reach your destination in the joy of the Lord, enjoying who you already are. Be who God created you to be. As you follow Him, He will process you from your promise to your ultimate purpose, and you will find yourself reigning in life by Christ Jesus.

Seeing Into Your Destiny

1. What type of "son" is led by the Spirit into his full inheritance?

2. What are the three biblical definitions of inheritance? How do they apply to your life?

3. Describe the primary incentive for spiritual growth in our lives.

4. When do we start reigning in life? Is the abundant life reserved for heaven?

5. List three things involved in the training process.

Profiles in Destiny

Profiles in Destiny

For two years after a rare autoimmune disease left her suddenly blind, Lisa Fittipaldi would wake up each morning, open her eyes and turn toward her bedroom window. "And then," she says, "it would dawn on me, like a bucket of ice being dumped on my head, that I could no longer see. I'd immediately go into a funk."

To try to lift her spirits, her husband, Al, encouraged Lisa to find a reason for living—reach out to friends, find a hobby or take up a cause, all to no avail. Finally, one day in 1995 after learning that psychologists often recommend art as therapy for depression, he brought home a set of watercolors. "I threw them at her and said, 'I don't care what you do—just do something!'" Al later recounted. Outraged by what she considered as the height of insensitivity, Lisa, who had never even drawn before, sketched a picture from memory of four colored glass jars. She captured their beauty with remarkable acuity.

Al was amazed at the awakening he saw in Lisa, so he encouraged her to enroll in a two-week art instruction class at Louisiana Tech University in Ruston, Louisiana. There Lisa learned basic painting techniques as well as strategies for memorizing her palettes and creating outlines. Ignoring the advice of those who said, "You're blind; you should do abstraction," she decided to focus on painting realism. Her art instructor was stunned by her ability to capture the "true inner spirit" of her subjects.

Three years later, her husband sent out press packets with samples of her work to a number of art galleries, catching the attention of the Florence Art Gallery in Dallas, Texas. At her first show she sold all fourteen of her paintings, firmly placing her on the pathway to success. Her paintings, primarily watercolors and oils, now hang in more than thirty galleries nationwide.

Chapter 8
Life
Designs

Several years ago Judith and I invested a considerable amount of energy into designing our dream home. Because of our passion for the great outdoors, we decided to purchase property just outside the city limits and build a stately, fully modernized, log and glass home. After months of searching for the perfect home site, we finally found it. Nestled high in a bay, overlooking a picturesque lake, it was the ideal setting for rural living. Once the property was located, we selected the blueprints and began the process of choosing cabinets, carpet, tile and roof color. It came together in a beautiful presentation that anyone would be delighted to live in. There was just one problem. We never got around to building it.

Many people invest energy into planning a life they never quite get around to building. Changing times, evolving roles, budding careers and revolving relationships force the abandonment of hopes, dreams and plans for the future. The passion for living is hard to maintain when everything around you is in a constant state of flux. After all, who wants to invest all of your energy into planning something that you cannot ever seem to build? The first time our plans are adjusted, we cringe. The second time our hopes are deferred, we sigh heavily and withdraw emotionally. The third time our plans fail, we stop dreaming of the future and began to focus on surviving the present. It's hard to maintain momentum when the direction in which you're supposed to move keeps changing. It's harder to build a life, a destiny, a relationship or a home when you are uncertain where your future lies.

How do you plan for the future in the midst of changing times?

You develop a course of action based upon your life *designs*— not necessarily your personal *desires*. But isn't that a blatant contradiction to what we saw earlier? Not necessarily. There are times when our *designs* and *desires* match up, and there are times when we must choose between our life designs and our human desires. (I've discovered that the incongruity between designs and desires is usually the result of adopting and adapting other peoples wishes for our lives rather than honestly acknowledging our own.) When we are forced to choose between designs and desires, we must consistently choose the way of divine design in order to discover true fulfillment in life.

Many times our inherent temperament and God-given talent conflict with our natural desires. Let me explain it like this. If you were divinely designed to touch other people through the gift of music, yet allow the opinions of others to direct you into a career considered to be infinitely more *stable*— thus adopting the need for stability as one of your primary desires—then you have developed an incongruity between designs and desires.

The short road to frustration is to focus on what you *think* you desire in life rather than on what you were created to *be* and to *do*.

Your Gifting Reveals Your Calling

A calling is a difficult concept to explain. I think of Louis Armstrong's definition of jazz. Somebody once asked him, "Mr. Armstrong, what is jazz?"

Louis replied, "Man, if you can explain it, you don't know what it is."

I think that is true of a calling. Sometimes you can't explain it. It is, as the old preachers used to say, "Better felt then telt. Better caught than taught." A calling is something to be experienced more than to be defined—when you find it, you know it. Trying to define a calling is as complicated as trying to describe the feeling of being in love. How can you elucidate love? Any scientific description you may come up with only reduces it down to something less than what it actually is. I don't have the words in my vocabulary to describe fully the emotions of being in love. But I sure knew what love felt like when I first spied Judith walking across the college campus in a T-shirt that said, "Go to Heaven, Tulsa!"

When you discover your calling, you know it; it becomes undeniable. I call it an "Aha!" moment. If you will seek the will of God, you will eventually encounter that moment when you experience a total awakening—an epiphany—the time when you fully know the purpose of your life. It will strike you as an undeniable truth, and you will intuitively realize it—mind, body and spirit. This is the instant when everything in your life comes into alignment. For a moment, at least, everything becomes clear. In spite of all the obstacles between you and your ultimate destination, beyond any reasonable doubt you know, "This is what I was born for!" You know instinctively that you are destined for this career, this woman, this man, this city, this church or this ministry—it is conviction born out of recognition of your purpose.

Whatever your calling—father, mother, businessperson, computer operator, lawyer, doctor, engineer, teacher, barber, cook or nurse—that calling will bring together your gifts, your abilities and God's highest and best use of your life. Any other use of your time and talent will be a lesser application of your God-given abilities and resources.

If God has gifted you in an area, the chances are more likely than not that your destiny lies in that area. I have often heard many well-meaning but spiritually naive leaders encourage people to abandon their natural gifting in search of a "higher" way of living. I've counseled with people who were taught by religion that they had to give up what they were naturally good at in order to find their calling. But what way could possibly be "higher" than to be a faithful steward over the gifts, talents and abilities that God intentionally selected for your life? I recently read the words of one author who said, "Don't confuse talent with calling. Just because you can doesn't mean you should." Although that may sound noble, sacrificial—even spiritual—on the surface, it is completely wrong! It is nothing more than a throwback to the asceticism of the early holiness pioneers who taught that we had to abandon the world in order to serve God, rather than glorifying Him openly, with our gifts and talents, before all men.

> **In our calling we have to choose; we must make our fortune either in this world or in the next, there is no middle way.**
>
> —*Marie Henri Beyle, French novelist*

Many gifted people fail to find their destiny, and they live miserable lives because of erroneous teaching that suggests you may have to give up doing what you love to do in order to follow God's calling. It sounds so "spiritual" to give up what you love to do in order to do God's will. But it was God who originally placed that "love to do" within you. The Creator of the universe took time to program your calling, gifting, talent and destiny into you. If you are good at something, get better at it and run with it! If God has given you the gift to play the violin, then don't throw your violin down. Glorify God with it.

When we create unhealthy, unbiblical distinctions between calling and gifting, and between the sacred and the secular, we create a religious system in which people believe the only way to serve God is through church-related ministry. In recent years I have discovered that ministry happens both inside and outside the local church. For too long churches have reduced ministry to the level of singing in the choir, teaching a Sunday school class or doing hospital visitation. As a result of this limited perspective, we have excluded many members in the body of Christ from fulfilling their calling and ministry in the marketplace.

In his notable book *That You May Prosper*, Ray Sutton shares an excellent point on the importance of viewing all of life as an opportunity for ministry: "There are no sacred/profane categories inherent in creation. The original garden had zones that were nearer to and further away from God, but everything everywhere was sacred. Corporate man, male and female, was to spread culture. What is culture? *Culture* comes from *cultus*, meaning worship. Thus [we are]...to transform the world into a place of worship, and thereby create true culture...[We are] making society into a proper place to worship God."[1]

When you enter your office on Monday morning, you may not be on your way to preach a revival, but you are entering one of the greatest harvest fields in the world today—the marketplace. Your career is the broadest platform you will ever have to communicate the grace and faithfulness of God. Even in a work environment that does not allow for personal witness you can share the evidence of God through your creativity, integrity and faithfulness.

A recent study indicates that no church can create enough meaningful jobs for all its members to serve in that setting. In fact, only a third of the membership of a local church can be given a significant job within the supportive structure of the church. On a national basis, that adds up to tens of millions of Christians. So if we believe that "serving the Lord" means working within the infrastructure of the local church, two-thirds of us are doomed to frustration and disappointment.

In Psalm 24, the psalmist declares, "The earth is the LORD's, and all its *fullness*, the world and those who dwell therein."[2]

William Wilberforce, a Member of Parliament for forty-five years, was one of Britain's great social reformers. Wilberforce was converted to Christ after an intense intellectual struggle a few years before he became a Member of Parliament. If he became a Christian, he reasoned, he would have to abandon his political aspirations and give up his circle of friends. He wanted both.

At a crucial time in that conflict, he sought the counsel of former slave trader John Newton, who was then an Anglican priest and the author of many hymns, including "Amazing Grace." In the words of biographer John Pollock, Newton "urged him not to cut himself out from his present circles or to retire from public life." Two years later Newton wrote to him, "It is hoped and believed that the Lord has raised you up for the good of His church and for the good of the nation."

Wilberforce took Newton's advice and stayed in politics, even though at that time in history "most evangelicals shunned public life as worldly."[3] He became the most influential figure in the movement resulting in the abolition of slavery in Britain.

A Child Shall Lead Them

My world shifted one day while reading a verse out of Proverbs. The wise man Solomon instructed parents to "train up a child in the way he should go, and when he is old he will not depart from it."[4] For most of my ministry I believed and taught that the way to which Solomon referred was, in fact, the godly way, the Christian way, the way of faith and conduct. Now, I'm not so sure that is what he meant. Let me qualify that statement before you consider me a heretic and burn this book as false doctrine.

Judith and I, perhaps more than many other parents, believe in instructing our children in righteousness. Christian living is not an option in our home. I fail to understand how some parents can require their children to wash their faces, eat their vegetables and attend school and then allow them to decide whether or not they want to go to church. In our home we believe that Christian living is infinitely more important than eating your vegetables. Neither are negotiable.

With that qualifier firmly hung in place, let me say that I believe Solomon was probably talking about the *way* called *destiny*, not the *way* of *Christianity*. While faithfully preparing their children for eternity, many parents fail to prepare them for destiny. My responsibility as a father is to assist my children in discovering their talents, gifts and abilities, and then training them in the best use of those qualities. One day I will give an account to God for the sense of purpose and usefulness that I have instilled in my three sons.

> **If the elders have no values, their children and grandchildren will turn out badly.**
>
> —*Chinese Proverb*

Judith and I have discovered that our children are remarkably distinct from each other in their talents and temperament. In addition to their physical dissimilarity, their aptitude is also unique. Though all three are accomplished students, our oldest son is probably the most academically gifted. A member of the International Baccalaureate Society, Terry III is already preparing for law school. He has maintained a perfect 4.0 grade point average since he was first enrolled in kindergarten. And yet he has little time for other people in his quest to learn and develop his intellect.

Our middle son, on the other hand, loves people and intuitively knows how to make them feel valued. Joshua is the friend we all long for. As my closest companion, he cannot bear to be left home when I am traveling the world or even going to the grocery store at the end of the block.

And then there is Tyler, the quintessential youngest child who is a gifted musician, a natural athlete and a nonstop comedian who makes us all laugh during the toughest moments of life. He completes our world.

My role, as a father, is to help each of my children discover their inherent gifting and ability and to coach them into greatness. To impose my personal desires on their lives would be to distort the life design that God has mapped out for them. Their success will not be determined by whether their mother and I are fulfilled in their career choices, marriage partners or income-earning ability; it will be judged according to the pleasure of the Lord in their lives. Therefore, I must train each of them to glorify God with the gifts He has graciously given them.

Follow the Design

Motivational guru Anthony Robbins says, "Every complex system, whether it's a factory tool or a computer or a human being, has to be congruent. Its parts have to work together; every action has to support every other action if it's going to work at peak level. If the parts of a machine try to go in two different directions at once, the machine will be out of sync and could eventually break down."[5]

We are, as human beings, exactly the same. We can dedicate our lives to developing certain disciplines, but if our learned actions do not fully support our God-given gifts, talents and abilities, we create emotional upheaval in our lives. If a person develops a discipline and achieves a goal, but finds himself not utilizing his inherent gifting, inner turmoil results. And inner turmoil always destroys your chance of long-term effectiveness. The same is true of inherited attitudes. If an individual is carrying around a certain disposition toward the purpose of his or her life, when, in fact, that person is "hard-wired" to produce something else, he will not find fulfillment unless he aligns his expectation with his gifting. To believe something false about yourself or to do something contrary to your natural gifting is to set yourself up for a systems breakdown. We must abandon false designs and wrong attitudes.

Consider the young lady I wrote about in *The Image Maker*.

> From the time Rebecca was a child, her father joked, "This is our future doctor." When she graduated from high school as the salutatorian, there was no question about where she would be going next. Eight years later, she once again stood on the stage to receive a diploma, this time for top honors at medical school. Shortly after her graduation, she entered her residency at Hillcrest Medical Center. Everything in her life seemed to be perfect, except for one small thing—she was deeply unhappy and thoroughly unfulfilled.
>
> In the midst of increasing depression, she scheduled a few days of rest and relaxation. Perhaps some time away from the daily grind would recharge her batteries and energize her to resume the frenetic pace in which she lived. Early the second morning she experienced a devastating emotional breakdown. It came while she was eating breakfast. When faced with nothing to do that day, she did not know how to respond. "Just how long has it been since my life wasn't perfectly mapped out for me?" she wondered.
>
> Frustrated with her lack of composure, she tried to pull herself together and couldn't. After three long days of soul-searching, with a trembling hand, she was finally able to reach for the telephone to call her father. The decision had been made; she was leaving her residency.[6]

Unfortunately, Rebecca is not alone in her delayed discovery. Like many others around us, she had become someone other than who she was created to be. Her desire to please her parents had dominated her detection of the divine design that the Creator had established for her life. She had settled for imitating life, rather than living life, by adopting values and desires that were not really her own. Our values determine our recognition, appreciation for and ultimately even the development of our gifts, talents and abilities.

Defining Your Values

Our success in life is the result of living faithful to the values we espouse.

So, what are *values*?

The late Milton Rokeach, one of the leading researchers and scholars in the field of "human values," once referred to a *value* as "an enduring belief." Simply put, values are the deep-seated, pervasive beliefs that influence every aspect of our lives. Our moral judgments, our responses to others and even our commitments to personal and spiritual goals are a result of the values we hold at the core of our being.

Values are the framework that holds our lives together. They determine our response in any given situation, minimizing the need to contemplate and analyze the options. When faced with choices in life we act on what we value, and what we value determines the course we take. The impact of our values is endless—from what we believe to where we live, how we raise our children, the career we choose and the hobbies we enjoy.

Our values set the parameters for the hundreds of decisions we make every day. They constitute the boundaries of our lives, the lines we will not cross as well as the options that drive us onward. And, quite frankly, the options that run counter to our value system are seldom acted upon. Let's face it. If we do not value the action we are faced with, we are not going to do it no matter how much we are nagged, provoked or even preached to.

> **The return to solid values is always hard...
> Distress, panic and hard times have marked
> our pathway in returning to solid values.**
>
> —*James Garfield, U.S. President*

One of the greatest struggles that many Christians encounter is knowing the "will of God." Scores of sincere people experience mental hernias over "decision making" as it relates to the will of God. I've come to the conclusion that our real struggle is not over the mystical will of God nearly as much as it is an internal struggle with our own personal value system. You see, once you decide what you value in life, decisions are much easier to make. You simply choose in accordance with your value system. After years of holding firm to the same values, the choices become sub-conscious ones—automatic responses. Our "core values" hold the power to determine our destiny. We suffer mediocrity or achieve success by what values we embrace.

This all sounds so nice and easy, so tried and true, so fail-proof—but it isn't. Why? Because we are human beings struggling to define what we really believe in, not computer systems acting upon a preprogrammed response. Here is the dilemma that many people face. If our values shape our lives, yet we're not clear what we value, then we're like a ship without a compass. It is impossible to chart a course without a directional reading on the destination. When we are uncertain of the destination, we forfeit the ability to measure success or failure.

The problem comes into play when we fail to clarify our values.

Values Clarification

Five times in Matthew 5 we hear the voice of Jesus contrasting His value system with the values of Moses. He challenged the prevailing beliefs of the Law and the Prophets, saying, "You have heard it said of old...but I say unto you." Everything the Jews held sacrosanct was scrutinized by the prophetic insight of Jesus as He pushed them inward—to the introspection of their own hearts. He clarified what really mattered in life.

The clarification of our values helps us to determine what we believe in and, therefore, what we expect out of life. So where do we begin? Perhaps more importantly, where do these values come from? Since values are "enduring beliefs," they are planted, like seeds, deep into the soil of our souls by the following means:

1. Your environment sets the stage for your value system. As a child you were raised in an environment that reinforced your identity and destiny or deconstructed your sense of well-being and purpose.

2. The authority figures that had influence over you instill either positive values or negative values into your life.

3. Your peers help to form your value system. Because of our desire to be accepted by others, we often find ourselves adopting values that are not our own just to feel the approval of others.

4. The religion in which you were raised shaped your values by revealing an accurate representation of God's character and nature or an inaccurate picture of God.

Every aspect of our lives is governed by the values we hold regarding that particular aspect. In order to grow and prosper in an area, we need to become consciously aware of the beliefs that we have about that area and how those beliefs impact our lives. If the beliefs are faulty, then we must challenge them and change them by the renewing of our minds.[7]

As you read this book you may desperately want to change the broken areas of your life, but you may be going about it all wrong. Perhaps you want to heal a broken marriage or spark a dying career or kick a bad habit, and you are frustrated with yourself because you feel powerless to change. You have deceived yourself into thinking that one morning you'll wake up and everything will be magically transformed. Wrong! Before your situation will ever improve, you may have to change your value system. And sometimes transformation only comes through the process of spiritual conflict.

In Ephesians 4:23, the Jerusalem Bible (Reader's Edition) says, "Your mind must be renewed by a spiritual revolution." Do you know what the object of a revolution is? The purpose of a revolution is to overthrow "governmental authority." If your mind has been ruled by the "governmental authority" of the kingdom of darkness, you can dethrone its power by renewing your mind to the truth of God's Word.

Casting Down Wrong Values

In ancient days, cities were built within massive walls, thereby protecting their citizens. When the city was under siege from an opposing army, the wall provided a formidable barricade that protected the city, holding the enemy at bay. Before any enemy force could expect to conquer a city, it first had to overcome that defensive barrier.

In addition to almost indestructible walls, towers were erected in strategic places throughout the city. During times of battle, warriors would position themselves in these stations, which towered above the surrounding wall. From these high vantage points they could see the location of the advancing troops and plan their strategy of defense and counterattack.

In order for the enemy to take the city, three objectives had to be accomplished. First, the wall had to be scaled or penetrated. Second, the towers had to be invaded. Third, the men of military strategy had to be killed or captured. After the military leaders were eliminated, then the general army was left without direction. Such was the strategy for first-century battles.

In 2 Corinthians 10, we see this very principle illustrated—not in a city, but in a mind.[8] Originally our minds were enemy-held territories. Our minds were the base of operation for the powers of this world. Rebellion, anger, lust, insecurity, intimidation and rejection ruled without resistance. These forces of darkness had complete control over our value systems. That's why Paul used military words and ideas that suggest physical combat, even though everything being described occurs in the mind.

Although the light of the glorious gospel has set us free, the enemy still attempts to operate through the strongholds that he has established. He seeks to rule our lives through lies we believed and the habits we adopted when we were under his control. The real battleground is at the point of the stronghold—the improper value system that rules our lives. In order to change our behavior effectively, we have to cast down the imagination and bring our thoughts captive to the image of Christ.

What are some of the values that have ruled your life? What are some of the positive values with which we should replace the negative ones? I've listed a few for your consideration. Please fill in the blanks with your own positive values.

Positive Values

❏ The will of God	❏ Adventure	❏ Integrity
❏ Loyalty	❏ Reputation	❏ Security
❏ Ministry	❏ Health	❏ Success
❏ Fulfillment	❏ Love	❏ Acceptance
❏ Intimacy	❏ Happiness	❏ Marriage
❏ Financial freedom	❏ Achievement	❏ Comfort
❏ Family	❏ Servanthood	❏ _____
❏ _____	❏ _____	❏ _____

Resolving Value Conflicts

I am convinced that almost every problem we have is rooted in a conflicted value system. When we fail to prioritize our values, we find ourselves being pulled apart by opposing values. Each value may be a healthy one but is mutually exclusive to the other. One value has to take precedence over the other. For example: If you place equal value on sex *and* freedom, you are a candidate for promiscuity. If you place equal value on adventure *and* security or on achievement *and* comfort, you are inviting emotional turmoil. Each of these values is appropriate, but you must prioritize one over the other.

Our relationships (family and otherwise) suffer when there is conflict in our value system. Emotional variances occur when we profess loyalty to one set of values and yet align ourselves with another set of values—when we do not practice what we believe. The Book of James warns us of this conflicted way of living: "Be doers of the word, and not hearers only, deceiving yourselves."[9] Please allow me to paraphrase it: "When we profess one set of values, and then live by another, we open the door to spiritual blindness and emotional confusion." Conversely, we find true fulfillment when we faithfully follow the things that really matter to us in life. A prudent pastor once told me, "Always let the main thing be the main thing." The greatest challenge we face in this area is in establishing a hierarchy of values and in following those that contain true worth.

One of my all-time favorite movies illustrates this principle in a classic scene. The movie was *City Slickers*, and the scene was played out between Billy Crystal, who played a city slicker out west on vacation, and Jack Palance, who played a crotchety old cowboy. This is how their conversation went:

Jack: "How old are you? Thirty-eight?"

Billy: "Thirty-nine."

Jack: "Yeah. You all come out here at about the same age. Same problems. Spend fifty weeks a year getting knots in your rope—then you think two weeks up here will untie them for you. None of you get it. *[pause]* Do you know what the secret of life is?"

Billy: "No, what?"

Jack: "It's this." *[He holds up his index finger]*

Billy: "Your finger?"

Jack: "One thing. Just one thing. You stick to that and everything else don't mean nothing."

Billy: "That's great, but what's the one thing?"

Jack: "That's what you've got to figure out."

Value Hierarchies

In order to clarify your values hierarchy, please list the top six priorities for your personal life in the space provided below.

1. _____

2. _____

3. _____

4. _____

5. _____

6. _____

Now, list the six priorities for your family in the space provided below.

1. _____

2. _____

3. _____

4. _____

5. _____

6. _____

Finally, please list the top six priorities for your career in the space provided below.

1. _____

2. _____

3. _____

4. _____

5. _____

6. _____

Do these three sets of values complement or contradict one another? What should be adjusted in order to bring congruence to the most important areas of your life?

Consider what matters most in your life from the categories

above, and list the top six values in a combined list. This is a simple way to begin the process of bringing congruence to your life.

1. _____

2. _____

3. _____

4. _____

5. _____

6. _____

There is an important formula that I have used to help others find the place of greatest fulfillment in life. It's so simple that it may seem superfluous, yet it really works:

Gifts, Talents and Abilities

$$+ \quad \text{Primary Values}$$
$$= \quad \text{Life Designs}$$

When we align our priorities with our divine abilities, we find the secret of our personal purpose in this world.

Consider your final values hierarchy for a moment. Do they support your gifts, talents and abilities? How do they complement or contradict your natural gifting? If your gifts, talents and abilities were given by God, and your values were formed by environment, authority figures, peers and religious instruction, which should take precedence over the other? The divine design should, of course! Your values are subject to change. Your inherent gifting is here to stay.

Life Maps

Standing in a cave on the eastern slopes of the Natal Drakensberg in southern Africa, I marveled at the colorful drawings etched into the side of the stone walls. The images were as interesting as they are ancient. Painted by the bushmen, they depict scenes of charging elephants, grazing giraffes and running antelope being chased by hunters carrying bows and arrows. Found on the walls of caves from Morocco to Zambia, these were not just images of an antiquated period in African history; they are maps of the lives that were lived all across the Dark Continent.

What is a "life map"? Just as a map presents places of interest in relation to one another, a life map displays significant events, values, decisions, talents, gifts and abilities in relation to each other. Since our lives are made up of stories, and our memories contain story and image form, the points on a life map usually also represent stories and images.

A life map is the modern equivalent of an ancient biblical memorial. The Old Testament is filled with the rich images of feasts, books, altars and boundaries, all of which were designed to provoke reflection in the hearts and minds of the Israelites. God warned them not to forget all the mighty works He performed in delivering them from all their enemies.[10] To forget the past is to repeat it. To forget the past is to abort the future. Life maps keep us from forgetting and aborting.

> ## To change an organization you have to change its stories.

> —*Richard Stone, head of The Storywork Institute,*
> *Orlando*

What is the purpose of a life map? Life maps give us a sense of the past while revealing the progress that we've made. Just as cartographers map the land in order to open the door to future progress, life maps help us to see the primary themes, needs, opportunities and challenges that characterize the pattern of our lives.

I want you to consider drawing a life map including your

past experiences and your future hopes. A life map can be a drawing of your childhood home filled with the significant events that helped to shape your identity. You could draw a road map, but in place of cities and highways, it should show images of important people in your life or stories of personal interests or patterns of a developing career. Perhaps you had to climb over a mountain of hardships to achieve a particularly rewarding objective. Include it. Be sure to incorporate images that represent your gifts, callings, talents and abilities.

Your life map should be clearly marked so other map readers can find their way around. This includes labeling the points of interest or importance that represent the stories from your life. You'll be amazed at the creative energy that will begin to flow when others question you about the images you've drawn. I've seen life maps that are so detailed and professional looking that they are later framed and hung in special places in the home. They are a wonderful help for remembering and presenting personal histories and future hopes.

Take a sheet of paper and draw your life map. I pray that you will begin to see the wonderful pattern of your life design. Your purpose and destiny are inherent in the person God created you to be.

Seeing Into Your Destiny

1. Consider the difference between your desires and your design. List these differences.

2. Explain how your gifting works in concert with your calling.

3. Did your childhood nurture your identity? How can you find mentoring for the areas in which you were never trained?

4. What influence do your values have on the choices you make in life? Do you ignore them or faithfully follow them?

5. What patterns emerge when you look at your life map? What actions do you need to take to create a better outcome in the future?

Section III

The Journey

Awakened
to
Destiny

Profiles in Destiny

Profiles in Destiny

Had you met her, you would have never thought her to be a hero. As a short, unassuming woman, she worked long, meticulous hours for little pay as a servant, and she appeared to be ill equipped for anything else, for she could neither read nor write. She had endured many hardships too, as was evident by her missing teeth, which had been knocked out, as well as by her narcoleptic condition, which resulted from a serious head injury. As unlikely a hero as she may have appeared to be, she was one of the greatest freedom fighters in history.

Seeing the injustice from which her people suffered, she vowed to deliver them, as Moses had done with the children of Israel. She was not the only one who noticed this parallel, for she was called the Moses of her people. She formed long and complicated escape routes for her enslaved people and personally led many of them to freedom. Her ability to command was so great that the great abolitionist John Brown said that she was a better officer than most whom he had seen and could command an army as successfully as she had led her small parties of fugitives. This statement rang true, because the unassuming woman, Harriet Tubman, managed to lead over three hundred slaves to their freedom through the Underground Railroad.

Several years after her daring rescue missions, Harriet paid a lawyer five dollars to research the will of her mother's first master. After searching through sixty-five years of records, he found the will in which her mother was legally emancipated. But since her mother was never informed of her right to go free, her family remained slaves until Harriet led them, one by one to freedom.

Chapter 9

Moving From
Disappointment to Destiny

Every child has an inner timetable for growth—a pattern unique to him... Growth is not steady, forward, upward progression. It is instead a switchback trail—three steps forward, two back, one around the bushes and a few simply standing before another forward leap.

—Dorothy Corkville
Briggs

Have you ever had a dream dissolve? Have you ever longed for something, prayed for it, put your heart, soul, mind and body into it, only to fail to see it come to pass? You had everything in order, and you just knew God wanted this to happen—yet it didn't.

If that describes your experience in life, let me encourage you. The world is filled with the stories of men and women who moved from disappointment to destiny because they refused to give up. What do Wolfgang Mozart, Albert Einstein, Vincent van Gogh and Michael Jordan have in common? They all failed miserably before eventually succeeding in the area in which they were most gifted.

For example, Mozart was told by Emperor Ferdinand that his opera *The Marriage of Figaro* contained "far too many notes" and was "too noisy." Van Gogh, whose paintings sell for millions today, sold only one painting in his lifetime. Einstein was considered a failure by his schoolmaster,

who said the young man would "never amount to much." And
Michael Jordan was cut from his freshman basketball team. Yet
each of these individuals continued to persevere until they succeeded in their respective fields.

Lord Byron, one of the most respected poets of all time, suffered with tuberculosis. Rather than embracing his status as a
victim, he persevered. Franklin Delano Roosevelt had polio, but
went on to become one of the greatest presidents in the history of
our nation. Self-pity was not welcome in his outlook on life. John
Milton could have felt sorry for himself when he went blind.
Instead, he wrote *Paradise Lost*. Thomas Edison's teacher told his
mother that he was "too dumb to learn." Wonder who the real
"dummy" was? When Handel wrote *Messiah*, he was living in
poverty and struggling with paralysis. But he refused to quit.

The only time we truly fail is when we fail to try. If you exercise faith and patience in your pursuit of destiny, it is only a matter
of time until you succeed in your endeavor or find a more significant path to walk on. In "The Psychology of Achievement," Brian
Tracy tells about four millionaires who made their fortunes by age
thirty-five. They were involved in an average of seventeen businesses before finding the one in which they eventually succeeded.[1]

Consider the story of one well-known man who was plagued
by defeat. In 1831 he failed in business and declared bankruptcy.
In 1832 he lost an election for the legislature. In 1834 his business failed again, and he declared bankruptcy a second time. The
following year his fiancée died. The year after he suffered a nervous breakdown. Two years later, in 1838, he was defeated in
another election. In 1843 he ran for the United States
Congress—and lost. In 1846 he made another bid for a seat in
Congress, and again he lost. Seven years later he entered a race
for the U.S. Senate and was defeated. In 1856 his name was
placed on the ballot for the vice presidency of the United States,
and he lost the election. In 1858 he ran for the presidency of the
United States, and he lost the election. In 1858 he ran for the
Senate and lost again. In 1860 he was elected president of the
United States. His name was Abraham Lincoln. In spite of this

horrifying series of setbacks, he went on to become one of the greatest statesmen of history. When commenting on his personal achievements, he said, "You cannot fail unless you quit."

We live in a culture that celebrates and elevates victimization. We are far more comfortable in blaming our friends, family, teachers, coaches, pastors and even God for why we have not succeeded in life. Our language is filled with self-pity. "If only I have more..." "If my teacher..." "If my parents..." "If my pastor..." "Why didn't they...?" Many people consider it their right to be a "victim." Therefore they continually define themselves by what they *lack* rather than by what they *have*. But our only real failure is that we have not recognized that failure is not a valid excuse for not succeeding!

Psychologist Dr. Joyce Brothers affirms, "The person interested in success has to learn to view failure as a healthy, inevitable part of the process of getting to the top."[2] Failure is only permanent when we stop trying to succeed. Regardless of the degree of our failure, or the consistency with which we fail, we can succeed, but only if we continue moving forward.

The Journey Inward

According to an ancient Chinese proverb, "The longest journey you will ever take is the one inward." Yet this journey is the most exciting one that any human being could ever make. The process of moving to the next level in any aspect of life begins internally, and eventually progresses to external transformation. The challenge to be like Christ and to succeed in our calling summons us to climb inner mountains of unbelief, cross inner valleys of passivity and apathy and forge inner rivers of rebellion and resistance.

I have traversed the soil of over sixty nations. As an outdoorsman, I have spent a great deal of time overcoming the challenges of the wild, yet I have found even the greatest hardships in international travel or wilderness survival to be quite simple compared to the journey inward—the pathway to wholeness. As psychologist Sheldon Kopp says, "All of the significant battles are waged within the self."[3] The call to experience that which "eye has not seen, nor ear heard" is inspiring to those who are courageous of heart, but it is dreadful to those are resistant to personal change.[4]

The process of discovering your destiny begins with a reality check—accepting where you are. And that can take courage. Where you are can be very different from where you want to be. Where you are can be very different from where you think you are. Where you are can be very different from where everyone else thinks you are. If you want to rise to the next level of your ordained destiny, you have to overcome the demons of denial so that you can deal with life on supernatural terms.

Supernatural power doesn't work where denial is present.

That's why Paul, when wrestling with the thorn in the flesh, said three times, "Lord, take this hindrance away from me."[5] The response Jesus gave was probably not one Paul was thrilled to hear. In essence, Jesus said, "Quit living in denial. Face where you are. My grace is sufficient for you to overcome, for My strength is made perfect in weakness." Some people never receive God's strength because they refuse to face the internal obstacles in their lives—their thorns in the flesh.

> **What evil is: Not as we thought, deeds that must be punished, but our lack of faith, our dishonest mood of denial.**
>
> —*W. H. Auden*

The challenges of life must be faced—not denied. Many people will never be delivered from the mess they are in until they are willing to get real and face where they are. Denial is not a divine gift. Denial is not a river flowing in Egypt. Denial is a dam that blocks the rivers of reality from flowing through your brain, preventing you from facing your circumstances and overcoming them. I have come to see denial as an acronym for:

D — don't

E — even

N — know

I — I

A — am

L — lying (to myself)[6]

You have to face where you are in order to get a bearing on where you are going.

Lest you mistake me for a pessimist, let me quickly add that I certainly do believe in the power of a positive confession. Fifteen years ago I discovered the power in aligning my personal words with the Word of God, and I have tried to remain faithful to that biblical principle. But I don't believe you have to lie about the obstacle you are facing. When you deny the reality of a sickness with which you are struggling, you leave no room for healing. To deny the marriage crisis in which you find yourself is to leave no room for restoration. To refute the hidden weakness in your life is to leave no room for grace. Grace and strength are made available in weakness.

Until you face it, you will never have the grace to displace it.

If your career is in a funk, don't lie to yourself about it. Stop pretending. Quit acting as if everything is fine. It isn't wrong to acknowledge, "This career stinks, and I need to get out of this thing. Lord, give me Your power to make a positive change."

It takes courage to admit failure. But we shouldn't let it embarrass us. We have all failed. We all go through difficult times. As a pastor, there is no doubt that I have preached some irrelevant messages, given poor counsel and even failed to lead at times. But the only way I was able to improve on my weaknesses was to face the failure of the previous week and move forward. I've learned to practice the process of failing forward.[7]

You will never advance until you honestly admit where you are. If you need to complete your degree in order to succeed in the field you have chosen, go back to college and get it. If your marriage is in a mess, admit it, humble yourself and get some help. If you are struggling to raise your children properly, there is no shame in acknowledging that you need training. If you are in debt and about to go under, admit you need help. Whatever the situation, stop denying it. Face it!

Embracing the Second Clause of Destiny

Being honest with where you are not only means that you have to face your failures; it also means that you have to acknowledge your desires. That can be tough to do if you were raised in a religious culture that taught you it is wrong to have ambition. As a young pastor, I was taught by well-meaning mentors that all ambition was an evil to be avoided. Not true! Let me clarify the issue for you. There is a difference between *selfish* ambition and *sanctified* ambition. Selfish ambition will only lead you down the road of pain, heartache and misery. It is a mortal enemy of servant leadership. It will use you up and spit you out without ever producing any sense of inner peace and fulfillment. And it will destroy the righteous relationships that God has set in your life. Sanctified ambition, however, is the desire to advance in life to the glory of God.

Sanctified ambition is the driving force that empowers us to achieve extraordinary results in life. When the young shepherd David first encountered Goliath in the valley of Elah, he asked the question, "What shall be done for the man who kills this Philistine and takes away the reproach from Israel?"[8] Upon hearing the answer, he turned to another and asked the very same question. Evidently, removing the reproach from Israel was not enough to light David's inner fire of determination—he wanted to know how the victory could benefit him individually. His driving ambition was to deliver the nation and to be personally blessed in the process. Thank God he didn't stop long enough to listen to the religious rhetoric of those who equate ambition with blasphemy.

Contrary to what monastic asceticism (the doctrine of poverty) teaches, there is nothing wrong in asking "What's in it for me?" Jesus always took His followers beyond the first clause of self-denial into the second clause of promise. The first clause always contains the call to servanthood; the second contains the promise to rule and reign with Him. Consider the following statements made by Jesus during His earthly ministry.

When Jesus called the disciples Andrew and Peter, He said, "Follow Me, and I will make you fishers of men."[9] The first clause contained the call to self-denial; the second revealed the opportunity to exchange a life of futility for and incredible adventure with eternal reward.

In Luke 6:38, Jesus instructed His followers to "give, and it will be given to you: good measure, pressed down, shaken together, and running over will be put into your bosom." The first clause contains the call to sacrifice; the second contains the promise of abundance.

In Luke 12:31, Jesus said, "But seek the kingdom of God, and all these things shall be added to you." Have you ever wondered why He didn't just say, "Seek the kingdom of God because it's good for you"? Period. But instead of leaving them alone in the first clause, Jesus promises the fulfillment of their deepest desires. The first clause contains the call to sacrifice; the second contains the incentive.

In Matthew 19:29, Jesus promised, "And everyone who has left houses or brothers or sisters or father or mother or wife or children or lands, for My name's sake, shall receive a hundredfold, and inherit eternal life." Once again the same pattern is present.

To live only in the first clause of destiny is to risk disempowering ourselves. It is the second clause that motivates most of us to take action. As one who has spent most of his adult life leading ministry teams, I have discovered that we always perform at the level at which we are motivated to perform in life. People rarely accomplish anything just because it is the *right* thing to do. A high level of motivation always creates a high level of performance. Conversely, low motivation creates low performance.

Granted, there are times when God calls us to serve in areas that hold no earthly reward. When He does, we must learn to respond in obedience and enthusiasm, knowing that a reward in heaven has been prepared for that very situation. The sanctified ambitions that we fail to fulfill in this life may only be postponed to the life to come, and the dreams that we die with may very well be reborn in the age to come.

What Makes Us Do Anything?

The subject of motivation is, at once, simple and complex. Simple, in that it explains much of what we see around us in human behavior. Complex because it poses contradictions. You may not be motivated particularly by the very thing that stirs me to action.

Probably the first question to be answered in a discussion of motivation is, "What makes us do anything?" Why are you reading this book? Why did you choose to start the process of developing your gifts, talents and abilities? Why do you get out of bed each day and go to work, knowing that you will encounter challenging situations? Each day brings with it an endless list of decisions to be made. The process of making those decisions is driven, in a large part, by the hope of a benefit or the fear of a consequence.

For example, I really enjoy eating Krispy Kreme doughnuts. I am only too happy to exchange my hard-earned money for the benefit of enjoying the flavor, texture and taste of what my wife calls "a redneck delicacy." (As you might guess, she doesn't fully share my enthusiasm for the "finer" things in life.) However, I have learned to limit my intake of these doughnuts for fear of the consequences of too much sugar and fat in my diet.

Literally every decision we make is filtered through this same process. We tend to act in direct proportion to our hopes and fears. The industrial psychologists have taken this further by defining the *fear of consequences* as "inner needs." Our need for sustenance, safety, security, belonging, recognition and a sense of growth and achievement become strong drivers (motivators) of behavior.

For example, the need to nourish ourselves is strong; hunger will drive us to extreme actions, particularly in the case of profound hunger. However, how does one explain a hunger strike? How can you explain the actions of someone who has died because they chose not to eat? A higher level need took over—the need to make a point about an issue that to the person was larger than life itself.

In dreams begins responsibility.

—William Butler Yeats, Irish poet

God often uses our needs as the motivation to draw us into the destiny He has designed for us. Just as our needs can communicate the action we should take in life, our innermost desires can also serve as the spiritual indicators of the gifts and talents with which He has uniquely equipped us. Our dreams motivate us to high levels of performance.

Facing the Dreamer

Are you dreaming in mono or stereo?

- To dream in mono is to selfishly seek your own path in life.

- To dream in stereo is to share in the purpose of God.

The dream God has for your life is more than an event or an achievement—it is you becoming who you were meant to be. God changes you to match the dream. God will use the dream to test you because He is more interested in what you become than in the dream becoming a reality.

Joseph had a dream at the age of seventeen, and it formed his outlook on the future. He saw his brothers bowing before him, but he wasn't ready for that dream to become a reality because his ambition had not been sanctified. In order to refine his motives, God allowed Joseph to be sold into slavery by his brothers and later to be falsely accused and thrown into an Egyptian prison. Joseph's future did not look promising. He must have endured many seasons of sadness and disappointment at the way his life had turned out. But the presence of God in his life sustained him. At some point on the journey, Joseph must have prayed something like this: "God, I don't know what is going on in my life. I don't know why all these unfair things have happened to me. But I know I can trust Your heart even when I don't understand Your hand. And that is enough."

Let's establish the difference between *dreams* and *fantasies*. Dreams sustain us during the dark night of the soul, but a person with a fantasy has no sustaining power. Why? Because power is resident in the dream, not necessarily in the dreamer. When you tap into the power of a dream, you discover the strength to succeed. And that strength will sustain the dreamer. But if you live in the realm of fantasy, there is no power to produce; therefore, when the fantasizer encounters disappointment, there is no motivating force—no divine unction—empowering that person to rise up and to continue the journey.

> **There can be no deep disappointment where there is not deep love.**
>
> —*Martin Luther King Jr.*

You say, "How do I know if what I have is a dream or a fantasy?" The testing will tell. And you can be sure that your dream will be tested. Dreams withstand the tests of life, but fantasies crumble.

Joseph's dream was tested in two ways: by barrenness and by

persecution. The first test involved his relationship with God, and the second involved his relationship with others. At some point on your way to destiny—on the journey toward your dream—you will encounter tests. And will have to settle issues with God and with other people involved in your life.

God will use the dream to test you, because He is more interested in what you become than in the dream becoming a reality.

Why Does God Allow Disappointment?

We've all asked the question at one time or another: Why does God allow disappointment in our lives? If He is a good Father who desires to give good gifts to His children, why does He allow our dreams to be tested? I can give you two primary reasons.

First, God allows our dreams to be tested because He intends for our character to match our dreams.

When God shows you His dream for your life, He is more interested in what you become than in what you accomplish. As we saw in a previous chapter, that is why God created us as human *beings*, not as human *doings*. Your destiny is attached to your identity more than it is attached to your activity.

But because we live in a world where success is measured by personal achievement and individual accomplishment, we measure our worth by activity rather than identity. That's why leaders often get nervous when things are quiet—when churches aren't exploding at the seams and when we are not receiving instant answers to our prayers. There are times when God allows everything to quiet down in our lives. He brings us into momentary seasons of holdback, momentary times of confinement—not because of judgment or because He is angry with us, but simply because He wants to bring our character up to the measure of our dreams. God wants us to know that He values us because of who we are, not because of what we do.

The baptism of Jesus wonderfully illustrates this principle. As John baptized Jesus in the Jordan River, the heavens opened, the Spirit descended on Him like a dove and the voice of the Father boomed out of heaven, "This is My beloved Son, in whom I am well pleased."[10] One day while considering this passage, it dawned on me that the Father acknowledged, honored, esteemed and affirmed Jesus before He ever performed His first miracle. His ministry had not even begun. I believe the Father was taking great care to show that His love for Jesus was not based on performance. It was, in essence, as if the Father said, "Let's settle one thing before Your ministry even begins; I acknowledge You as My beloved Son. I love You unconditionally. I honor You before Your peers. I am proud to be Your Dad."

Sometimes we need to remind ourselves that our worth in the eyes of the Father and the favor He bestows on us are not based upon how well we perform. It is predicated upon one thing—who we are. He loves us even if we struggle through life without fulfilling our purpose. He loves us if we cycle from failure to failure, and disappointment to disappointment. It's not our responsibility to uphold God's reputation throughout all of the earth. Thank God, it is not my responsibility to be the model of a perfect leader or a perfect pastor. It is my responsibility to be God's son, to delight in my sonship, to take my identity from His Fatherhood and to be obedient to His passion for my life. If I do that, everything in my life is successful no matter what it looks like to others. God is more interested in what we become than in what we accomplish.

Second, God allows disappointment in our lives to prove that we can't get there on our own.

A God-given dream is always bigger than we are, and it cannot be reached in our own strength. That is why, when heaven inspires a dream, we need God to help make it become reality.

Whatever your dream—if it is in politics, business, athletics, academics or medicine...if it is to be a leader in the community, to have a great marriage and raise sane children—God will allow it to be tested. He will do this to prove that you need Him to make the dream a reality.

You cannot bring your dream to pass on your own without sacrificing some part of the dream. If you reach the destination without your wife, without your husband, without your children, without character, without health, without sanity—then you haven't reached the dream. While you may achieve whatever you are reaching for, it may not be God's dream for your life; God wants you to arrive there with every other good thing still attached.

We live in a disposable generation where people are willing to sacrifice whatever they think is necessary in order to reach their goals. Marriages are sacrificed on the altar of ambition. Children are sacrificed before the shrine of selfishness. Health is sacrificed at the expense of drive and determination. Sometimes morals and values are sacrificed—all to reach the ultimate pinnacle of success. But that is not the way of the kingdom. That is not God's dream for our lives.

The way of the kingdom is found in the lives of the great patriarchs of the Bible. When these great men reached their dreams, they were surrounded by their families and those whom God had put in their lives. They were blessed with every good thing. And when they had fulfilled their purpose, they laid down in peace and were gathered to their fathers. They did not die frustrated because of unfulfilled expectations. They had accomplished everything that God had put into their hearts.

God gives the dream, but He also gives us families and responsibilities. He does not ask us to sacrifice one or the other. I have a friend who has waited years to have her first novel published—all the while working with pastors and teachers as a ghostwriter and seeing their works published. There are times when she wishes she had more time for her own writing, but there are legitimate demands on her time from a husband and children as well as the writing that brings in the income that helps pay the bills.

She often has to remind herself, "God knew I was married and had children when He gave me this dream—when He called me to write—and I have to believe that He knows what He's doing." She has never felt comfortable sacrificing time with her family in order to pursue her dream of being a published author. God gave her both the family and the dream. And she's still waiting...closer today than yesterday.

> **Despair is a narcotic. It lulls the mind into indifference.**

—*Charlie Chaplin*

Success is a package, and God will allow you to be tested to prove that you can't get there without Him. You can't get there without the people you love and the people who love you. So prepare for your dream to be challenged through the bitter pain of disappointment.

Disappointment simply means, "Not as planned or appointed." One of our greatest struggles in life is with issues that do not go as we planned. When our hopes and dreams fail to materialize within the time frame we have allotted for them, we grow faint of heart. Our disappointment is generally directed at one of the following: God, others, ourselves or circumstances. Let's explore all the usual suspects.

Disappointment With God

As much as we try to deny it, much of our disappointment is directed at God when He doesn't measure up to our expectations or perceptions. Failing to understand His true nature and character, we harbor religious images (spiritual fables) of God. And when we perceive God to be anything other than who He is, we set ourselves up for disappointment.

Another reason people are disappointed with God is because they have a fantasy about something and have convinced themselves that it was from God. Then they blame Him when whatever they believed for doesn't come to pass.

A misunderstanding of the Scripture that says that God is no respecter of persons can also lead to disappointment.[11] Some people believe that Scripture means that God is a socialist or even an equal opportunity employer—but He isn't. God doesn't give everyone the same talent or gift—He gives some ten talents, others five and others one.

Somehow we have developed this touchy-feely image of God in our postmodern culture, and we think that God is *fair*. No, He isn't. He is *just*. To illustrate this, Jesus taught the parable of the manager who hired one employee at 9 A.M., another at 1 P.M. and another at 5 P.M.—only to pay them the same wage at the end of the day.[12] This parable illustrates that God is sovereign, working with unlimited information, while we are working with limited insight. He knows more about us than we know about ourselves. And He knows more about what it will take to get us to our intended destination.

God determines your destiny, and He alone knows exactly what you need to accomplish your life's purpose. So if He gives you a gift, use it. And if He withholds something you want, live without it. God always has your best interest at heart, which is why He chooses our inheritance for us.[13] If you are disappointed with God, surrender your agenda and buy into God's plan for your life.

Disappointment With Others

Another area where we frequently experience disappointment is disappointment with others. Other people can shatter your dream, hinder it or belittle it. People you love can disappoint you. It happened to the apostle Paul more than once. He sent a young disciple named John Mark home because he didn't think Mark was up to the task. Later, Mark did end up being a powerful man of God, but at the time Paul was very disappointed with him. Then there was Demas—you can hear the pain in Paul's words when he writes, "Demas has forsaken me, having loved this present world, and has departed for Thessalonica."[14]

When someone we love and trust disappoints us, the first emotion we experience is shock. We can't believe that person betrayed us. The biggest shock is not that the dream didn't come to pass, but that the person who was beside us—the person we loved—disappointed us. We all struggle with disappointment in others. And it really shouldn't surprise us.

If you put your trust in people, you are guaranteed to be disappointed. At some point or another, someone will let you down and disappoint you deeply. That is why Paul instructed us not to place any confidence in the flesh.[15] That means your flesh, my flesh, husband flesh, wife flesh, parental flesh, pastoral flesh—every kind of flesh!

The prophet Jeremiah warned us of the danger of trusting in someone other than God when he said, "Cursed is the man who trusts in man and makes flesh his strength."[16] If you are trusting in someone or something other then God to bring you happiness and hope, you are a candidate for continual disappointment.

I am convinced that most relational failures happen because of two things: unrealized expectations and unrealistic expectations. Many times our disappointment with others is a result of unrealistic expectations. We thought our expectations were legitimate, but when they were unrealized, we fell into despair and disappointment. No one in the universe is capable of meeting all of our needs. God reserves that place for Himself.

Jesus was never disappointed in people even though He surrounded Himself with some pretty rough characters. When we see paintings or statues of the disciples, they all look so holy. You never see a painting of Peter with a four-letter word coming out of his mouth. You never see a painting of James frowning and pointing a finger at someone. We get the wrong image of what these guys were like. They were scoundrels and rascals—some were fishermen, one was a tax collector and one was a thief. But Jesus was never disappointed with them. He challenged them. He rebuked them. But He never said, "You guys are really disappointing me." Jesus knew what was in the heart of man, and He had no false expectations. He had no illusions about the men he chose to be His disciples. Therefore, He had no disappointments.

Simon Peter betrayed Jesus, but Jesus didn't shake His head sadly and say, "Peter…Peter…you really disappointed Me this time." Jesus knew Peter's capacity for betrayal and chose him anyhow. He loved him. He forgave him. He restored him. He brought Peter from disappointment back to destiny.

Disappointment in Ourselves

The third target of disappointment is when we are disappointed in ourselves. This usually happens when we are honest enough to admit that neither God nor others are responsible for our failures.

Many times we are disappointed the most in our own actions and choices. It can be harder to forgive yourself than anyone else. That's the time to remember that God is still in control. Your circumstances do not control God. God chose you knowing your capacity for failure—and He loves you. That is why you are never going to hear the Father say, "I am disappointed in you." Your failure didn't catch God by surprise. He knew you were going to blow it. And He still loved you and affirmed you in advance, just as He loves and affirms you through the process of restoration and will continue to love and affirm after you have been restored.

Disappointment in Our Circumstances

Circumstances can bring great disappointment. There are times when we can't find anyone or anything to blame—except the pain of being human. We know that God is good. We know that the people around us did everything right. We know that it wasn't any failure of our own. It was simply the circumstances. We live in a sin-ravaged, sin-cursed world. Daily we fight an enemy who wants to destroy us, ruin our marriage, abort our prosperity or paralyze our ministry. We were born in war. We live in war. We will die in war. Until Jesus comes back and ends the war, we are consigned to life on a battlefield—and casualties often occur. People get sick. Some die. Some go bankrupt. Some lose ministries. Life leads us through many transitional processes, but through it all, we can be confident in the fact that we are sons and daughters of the Most High God.

There is a remarkable story found in 1 Samuel, chapters 1 and 2. It is the story of a woman who went from having a dream through great disappointment and, ultimately, to her destiny. Her name was Hannah.

Hannah's dream was to have a child. In particular, she wanted a son. This was complicated by the fact her husband had two wives. In this environment, rife with competition, jealousy, strife and hurt, we hear the pathos in these words, *"Hannah had no children."* Barrenness in ancient times was the ultimate tragedy for a married woman. Every man wanted a male heir to perpetuate his name and to inherit his estate. Barrenness was also considered a sign of divine punishment—of spiritual rejection. And yet year after year, Hannah struggled with an unfulfilled dream, a misunderstanding husband, a heartless rival and devastating disappointment.

Here was a woman torn by two conflicts—at times she felt that God was punishing her for something of which she was unaware; other times she felt that her husband was disappointed in her for not providing the son for which she—and he—desperately longed. In spite of her husband's reassurance and love, Hannah felt less than a whole woman because of her barrenness. But Hannah had a dream. She believed for a son. And in spite of her misery, shame, ridicule, rejection and embarrassment, the power of that dream worked in her life, and that dream sustained her.

Hannah sets a wonderful example for us. First, she is brutally honest about her true feelings. She doesn't try to put on a spiritual show for anyone and say, "Well, praise God, it doesn't matter if I have children or not. I'm just fine." She admitted that she was deeply troubled, bitter and in great anguish and grief. But Hannah also prayed. In her disappointment and grief, she did not turn away from God.

> **If you shoot for the stars and hit the moon, it's OK. But you've got to shoot for something. A lot of people don't even shoot.**

> —*Robert Townsend*

Hannah's story reminds us of God's unswerving faithfulness. In the course of time, Hannah conceived and gave birth to a son. When her dream became a reality, she didn't forget God. Hannah kept her promise, and she dedicated the child Samuel to the Lord. She weaned him at the age of three, as Hebrew mothers did, and took him to the temple. Then God blessed her with five more children. By trusting God and staying faithful during times of temptation, testing and trial, Hannah moved from a dream through disappointment and into her destiny.

Slam-Time Living

Friedrich Nietzsche once said, "Along the journey we commonly forget its goal. Almost every vocation is chosen and entered as a means to a purpose but is ultimately continued as a final purpose in itself. Forgetting our objectives is the most frequent stupidity in which we indulge ourselves."[17] Regardless of why your dream has been delayed or who is responsible for keeping it from coming to pass, there are some things you can do to generate momentum. I am a firm believer in "Slam-Time Living." Consider the following acronym I created as a pattern for your life.

- **S**eek God's will

- **L**ive your passion

- **A**cquire a mentor

- **M**aintain your focus

- **T**ake healthy risks

- **I**nspire yourself

- **M**aster your goals

- **E**njoy the journey

Lance Armstrong is a man who has mastered the principles contained within this chapter. The three-time winner of the Tour de France is a classic example of one who moved from a dream through a disappointment and eventually into his destiny.

In 1996, Lance Armstrong was a top-rated cyclist who appeared to be on the threshold of achieving his ultimate dream to compete in the Tour de France race. In the world of competitive cycling, this race is the supreme test of strength and endurance. For twenty-two days, twenty different stages and 2,286 miles, some of the world's most conditioned athletes race over hills and valleys, through towns and cities to win the coveted title.

And then tragedy struck.

Suddenly, without warning, Lance began coughing up blood and experiencing headaches, blurred vision and soreness in the groin area. When the tests came back from the doctor's office, he was stunned. He had an aggressive form of testicular cancer. By the time it was discovered, it had already worked its way into his abdomen, lungs and even his brain. It was reported that there were eleven masses in his lungs alone, some the size of golf balls. His brain was invaded by two malignancies. He was given a 50 percent chance of survival.

Attacking the cancer as if it were nothing more than another cycling challenge, Lance threw off the disappointment and developed a plan of action. From brain surgery to chemotherapy, he did everything possible and refused to give in to depression, resignation or failure. Five short months after his diagnosis, he began training to resume his career as a competitive cyclist. Following his miraculous recovery, Lance went on to score stunning victories at the Tour de Luxumbourg, the Rheinland-Pfalz Fundfarht in Germany and the Cascade Classic in Oregon. Shortly thereafter, he placed in the top four in the Tour of Holland and the Tour of Spain, one of the three most elite races in the world! In 1999 his dream finally became reality when he entered the Tour de France race and cycled to his destiny with a seven-minute, thirty-seven-second lead over the nearest competitor. In two short years he came back from the brink of death to win the Tour de France![18] Not satisfied, he repeated his performance in 2000 and 2001, making him the only competitor in the history of the sport to win the coveted title three consecutive years.

Just as the men and women of this chapter moved from a dream through a devastating disappointment and finally to their destiny, so can you. But you have to be willing to persevere. Overcoming the challenges of life is not as easy as following a twelve-step process for success—it is about releasing the need to succeed. When nothing else will satisfy you but the fulfillment of your dreams, you have begun the journey toward your destiny.

Seeing Into Your Destiny

1. Have you ever experienced a disappointing setback in life? How did you move beyond it?

2. What is your perspective on failure? Do you view it as an enemy or an opportunity?

3. Explain the difference between selfish ambition and sanctified ambition. Has your ambition been sanctified? How so?

4. Why does God allow disappointment? What should our response be?

5. Define "Slam-Time Living." Where are you in the process?

Profiles in Destiny

Profiles in Destiny

The atmosphere was tense in Orleans, France, as a starving, disgruntled militia tried to defend the city against an army with superior numbers, arms and technology. This depressed the commanders and officers, for if Orleans fell to the enemy, the invaders would conquer all of France. As the months dragged on, the situation only seemed to worsen until one day in A.D. 1429.

On this day, rumors began to spread like wildfire that a new general had arrived with a mission to save Orleans and ultimately all of France. As the new general marched through the streets with an army, a new sense of life flowed through the town. This inspiration, caused by one person, transformed a disillusioned militia into an uncompromising army that defeated the enemy's advance and saved the city.

But this was only the beginning of the commander's exploits. The "Maid of Orleans," as she was called, was almost single-handedly responsible for the rebirth of the French Army and the reemergence of France as a world power. Even her death, a martyr-like execution by the British, moved both her friends and enemies to seek her cause.

All of this was a result of a vision, literally. Responding to what she believed to be the voice of God, a seventeen-year-old peasant girl named Joan of Arc managed to turn the tide of the Hundred Years' War and expel the British Empire from France—forever.

Chapter 10
Living at the Next Level

The young man moved his caffé latte to one side and leaned across the table, "I just want to know what my life's purpose is. I'm so confused. I know there is something that I'm supposed to be doing, but I don't know what it is. If I could get some clarity, then I know I could take action." The lines deepened on his brow, and his face took on a worried look. "I feel like I've hit the wall, and I have nowhere left to turn."

These were not the words of someone trying to find out where to begin in life. They were spoken by a young man who was convinced he had taken a wrong turn. At thirty-seven years of age, he had recently celebrated thirteen years with a computer software design company that had gone "public," leaving him with a net worth of five million dollars. On the verge of retirement, he had everything he wanted in life—a magnificent home, a gorgeous wife and a healthy child. But he was emotionally bankrupt. He had poured his life into a career path that held little value for him, and somewhere along the way he had forsaken the things that really mattered. Life had become mundane—a series of days running into weeks, months and years. He had stopped moving forward spiritually, emotionally and relationally.

As I reflected on his predicament, I was reminded of the number of times I've heard the same story from the type people most of us try to emulate: athletes, entertainers, Christian leaders and successful CEOs. Regardless of the profession, the pattern is the same. The unsuccessful man sees his dream as the greatest goal life has to offer, whereas the man who has achieved his dream realizes that there is more to be experienced in life. Looking back on what we could have done differently—should have done differently—we see the stark contrast between the choices that seemed so inconsequential at the time: the decision to cut short a family vacation in order to finish a project at the office; the family meals that were missed because of an opportunity to score points with the boss by working late; the family prayer time that was postponed because we were just too tired to lead anyone anywhere at the end of another hard day—these are opportunities that were missed because of a misunderstanding regarding what success actually is.

Achieving a lifelong dream does not guarantee success or inner fulfillment. Think about what happened with the legendary basketball player Michael Jordan. After achieving superstar status by breaking a number of NBA records, he decided to retire from basketball and become a baseball player. Following a pathetic start in the minor leagues, he gave up baseball and returned to his first love, basketball. A couple of years later he retired…the second time. But Michael just can't seem to stay away from the game. He came out of retirement to play again, this time with the Washington Wizards. At thirty-eight years of age, he experienced an incredible comeback! In Michael's case, as in each of ours, we can see that success is not a final destination—it is a lifelong journey.

How do you measure success?

We are all designed with different gifts, and we desire different outcomes in life. That's what makes building a healthy marriage so challenging. In a marriage we not only have the challenge of discovering and defining our own personal gifts and desires; we now have to support and encourage another individual who is on the same journey with a slightly different destination. The definition of success is not the same for any two individuals. Why? Because it is based upon personal gifts and individual desires, and both are as unique as the fingerprints with which you were born.

So, what exactly is success?

Success can be defined as:

1. Knowing God
2. Understanding yourself
3. Discovering your purpose
4. Fulfilling your potential
5. Serving others
6. Enjoying the journey

As you can see by this definition, the journey is unending. You cannot exhaust any one of the six components above, no matter how long you live or in what career you decide to invest your energies. It will take a lifetime to know God, understand yourself, discover your purpose, fulfill your potential and serve others. And in this context, you can be successful every day of your life, not simply by reaching some eventual destination. When you see success as a lifelong journey, you will never feel defeated by the challenges you encounter and the obstacles that seem to delay you temporarily.

Victory belongs to the most persevering.

—Napoleon Bonaparte

As we saw in the previous chapter, success is never determined by what we have accomplished. It is measured by who we have become and how we have responded to the challenges and opportunities with which we have been presented. Pioneer aviator Charles Lindbergh once said, "Success is not measured by what a man accomplishes, but by the opposition he has encountered and the courage by which he maintained the struggle against overwhelming odds." Success is a matter of continuing the journey even when you feel like giving up.

The kingdom calls us onward and upward, out of the comfort of predictability and into the glorious unknown. As we live and move and find our being in Jesus Christ, we are led progressively into the process of personal transformation. This process qualifies us to embrace and experience the next level of God's glory.

Getting Unstuck

In spite of the call to live at the next level, we all experience those frustrating times when we do not seem to be making any measurable progress. You know what I mean. We've all had those days, weeks and even months when we expend our energy on activity that seems to lack destiny. In spite of our best efforts we find ourselves generating motion without creating momentum. These are the times when we are tempted to give up—to walk away from friends, families, careers, churches and even to abandon our hopes and dreams for the future. The good news is that we don't have to remain in that place, at least not for very long. There are certain principles that, when followed, will bring us back into the flow of God's purpose.

What Is the Next Level?

Dr. Lawrence Kohlberg of Harvard has led the way in research in moral education and social development. In his studies, he discovered that a healthy mature person develops through three levels of personal growth. Not only do these three levels pertain to our moral and social development, but they also can be applied to spiritual growth and maturity.

Level One—Birth to about age ten

This is the totally self-centered stage. All issues and choices are viewed in terms of personal, physical or pleasurable results. The rules of the game are: "If I am rewarded as I desire, my conduct must be good. If I don't get what I want, then I must be behaving wrong." According to this way of thinking, the end justifies the means. Daily, I deal with persons of all ages who have not grown out of this stage. Their motto is: "Do your own thing." They are totally self-centered egotists—committed to getting their own way regardless of whom they hurt in the process.

Level Two—Ages ten to fourteen

At this stage we begin to consider what others think of us. Choices are based on whether they will please others or are approved by others. Peer pressure begins to exert an enormous influence. The status quo becomes important. I frequently encounter persons of all ages still hung up at this level. "Everybody is doing it" becomes the mantra for mediocrity.

Level Three—Begins anytime after the late teens

At this level a person isn't trying just to please self or others; he is concerned with doing what is right. Internal convictions become important. Morality is based on principle, not on force as in level one or acceptance as in level two. Honesty is based on values, not on what parents say or others think.

The driving force for selfless living, at this level, is what Stephen Covey calls "Principle-Centered Leadership."[1] One college freshmen expressed it well when she wrote her dad: "I have decided that my conduct will not be based on whom I am with, but on who I am and what I believe."

Psychologists have concluded that there are three motivational factors in life: self-preservation, self-gratification and self-glorification. In each instance, note the use of the word *self*. I am convinced that any motivation generated because of "self" is fleeting and, ultimately, unfulfilling. The highest level of satisfaction in life comes in knowing that you have given your life away freely and that you have been instrumental in making the world a better place for others. A wise man once said, "People who live for themselves are in a mighty small business."

On level three we move from "What's in it for me?" to "What can we do to transform our sphere of influence?" We mature from the personal experience of living for ourselves to the corporate experience of living for others, from "me, my and mine" to "we, us and ours." This is the level where we begin to realize that even though each person we encounter in life has a unique base of gifts, passions and talents, our destinies are inter-connected—especially in the kingdom of God. Giving is the highest level of living.

> In externals we advance with lightning express speed, in modes of thought and sympathy we lumber on in stagecoach fashion.
>
> —*Frances E. Willard*

On What Level Are You?

The most important questions you should be considering right now are: How do you get to that next level? How do you get to that next level of a loving marriage relationship? How do you get to the next level of career advancement? How do you get to that next level of academic excellence or musical accomplishment? What separates those who are high-performance achievers from those who are just in the field? What separates a hero from a zero? What keeps some people at the level of mediocrity in life while others excel and advance in the kingdom of God and prosper in all that they do?

Remember, as I mentioned earlier, destiny is more than a

destination—it is a journey in which each day counts. You don't suddenly become successful when you arrive at a particular status in life. But that doesn't mean that we should blindly stumble along life's path without a destination in mind. You cannot become who God intends for you to be without having a picture of who that person is and what that person is called to do. I am convinced that those who travel the path of destiny God has purposed for them are motivated by at least six factors. I've identified them in the chart on the next page as the "The Building Blocks of Next-Level Living." These principles are character, core values, competencies, cause, compassion and courage.

As we examine these building blocks, personalize the chart by answering the questions in the space provided in each block.

Developing Your Character

When you look in the mirror each morning do you see a person of possibility, potential, purpose and power? Do you see a person who is loved, accepted, necessary and needed? Or do you see something far different?

At one time or another, and in one way or another, we ask the question, "Who am I?" Our answer to that question will shape our thoughts, emotions, actions and future. The way we see ourselves determines what we expect from life and at what level we perform in life. Some people never discover who they really are because they keep looking horizontally instead of vertically. They search for their identity in a dysfunctional world where *identity crisis* seems to be a rite of passage, rather than looking to the One who created each individual as a part of His grand design. The discovery of who we really are begins with the affirmation of this single truth: Our real identity is in God, not in the world. Any description of your life that is not based upon God's appraisal is illusionary, condescending and incomplete.

Character is the combination of identity and lifestyle. Since we've already examined the importance of defining who we are,

The Building Blocks of Next-Level Living[2]

> **COURAGE**
> *What action can you take?*
> _____

> **COMPASSION**
> *For whom do you care?*
> _____

> **CAUSE**
> *To what can you give your life?*
> _____

> **COMPETENCIES**
> *What are you capable of achieving?*
> _____

> **CORE VALUES**
> *In what do you believe?*
> _____

> **CHARACTER**
> *Who are you, and how do you behave?*
> _____

let's take a look at the importance of building character of lifestyle.

What is character? The person who believes in moral absolutes may find that question somewhat trite, but many people have embraced moral relativism to such a degree that they no longer understand the nature of character. *Character* is defined as "the pattern of behavior or personality found in a group; moral constitution." Therefore, character is the inner structure of our lives that undergirds our hope, dreams, desires and ambitions.

There are many things in life over which we have absolutely no control—parents, talent, upbringing and IQ among them—but we always have the right to choose our character. As the Greek philosopher Epictetus said, "No person is free who is not master of himself." Personal freedom is the result of mastering the development of character in our lives.

Our character forms our responses to the circumstances of life. That which is born of the fruit of the Spirit empowers us to stand strong when the winds of adversity blow. That which is born of carnal living weakens our purpose and our witness. Other people may be *impressed* by our talents, but they are *influenced* by our character.

Defining Your Core Values

As we saw in chapter nine, your core values are the principles that govern your belief system and your behavior. They are, in essence, the promise you make to yourself and others about how you intend to live your life. Core values become the point of reference by which we measure the success of our lives.

Many people struggle to define the meaning of success. But success is simply doing what you are called to do in a way that is compatible with your core values. In other words, success is a matter of doing the right thing—not simply doing things right. If we are successful in something that is incongruent with our core values, then we are not really successful.

Determining Your Competencies

Competencies are the skills, knowledge and abilities that are required to excel in your God-ordained destiny. Identifying one's areas of weakness both accurately and precisely is the first and, arguably, most important step toward developing those areas. The next step is to create and document an action plan. For each competency, list specific behavioral objectives and create a written plan outlining all the activities you intend to use toward meeting those objectives. These activities may be as simple as reading a book on time management or increasing your prayer and Bible study disciplines. The third step is to create a system that provides accountability for your actions and reactions.

Building on the principles you've just read, the following paragraphs contain a practical three-step program that has enabled many people just like you to discover and develop their core competencies.

Step 1: Identify the areas that need improvement.

Gather information on your strengths and weaknesses. There are a number of effective assessment tools available, or you may want to assess your abilities in an informal way, using your pastor, employer and/or coworkers to give you feedback on the strengths and weaknesses they see in you. Feedback you have received in the past outside of work (for example, within your family, at school or with friends) may also provide a valuable source of corroborating information to take into consideration when identifying your strengths and weaknesses.

Using the chart on page 203, list your strengths and weaknesses. Do not worry about assigning a priority ranking to these strengths and weaknesses in this first step.

Process through the information. Making a concerted effort to gather feedback on your weaknesses from such a potentially diverse array of sources certainly has the potential to be a rather *humbling* experience. It is important to recognize that not every behavior or competency identified by a given individual or assessment tool as a weakness will necessarily be a weakness. You will need to *distill* the vast amount of information you have at your disposal to identify a small number of competencies (two or three at most) upon which you can focus your efforts.

Keep in mind that the feedback you receive from individuals

will depend on a variety of organizational and interpersonal issues, as well as that individual's personal belief about what constitutes effective vs. ineffective behavior. Those beliefs may vary enormously from individual to individual.

When you have processed all the information you have received, in the column headed "Priority Ranking" in the chart, assign a number to each strength and weakness, beginning with #1 as the most obvious strength or the most critical weakness needing to be changed. It will be helpful for you to identify those strengths that God has allowed you to develop as giftings to be used in fulfilling your destiny. It will also be important to identify the weaknesses most important for you to change.

Consider the areas that need to be improved. Spend some time reflecting on the information you have gathered. There is no more valuable source of information about your own behaviors, strengths and weaknesses than the Holy Spirit. Ask Him to reveal the *blind* spots in your life. It is important that you strive to be honest and as objective as possible in assessing yourself. It is also important that you receive and acknowledge feedback from other sources openly and nondefensively. Reflect upon the results of your assessments and the feedback you receive from others. In some cases, you may feel that what others have rated as a weakness is not a weakness. If so, then you need to reflect upon why they *perceive* it as a weakness.

A given competency is really a mosaic of different behaviors that manifest themselves in your work performance in a number of different ways. It is unlikely that you are weak on all the behaviors relevant to a given competency.

Decide how many of the weaknesses listed in the chart on page 203 are affecting several of your competencies in a negative way. These are the most important weaknesses for you to change immediately.

Step 2: Create an action plan for learning.

Create or identify several learning activities. Now it is time to take action. Using the chart on page 203, list the specific behaviors (action steps) you will develop to overcome that weakness. (For example, procrastination may be affecting your competencies in your career, in your relationships and in your ability to reach important goals. Deciding to learn to manage your time more effectively by using a time-management system is a behavior that will help you overcome your tendency to procrastinate.) Some of the activities will be actual behaviors that you use to practice on the job (e.g., "Smile more frequently" or "Speak slowly and clearly"). Other activities will involve pursuing additional resources with the intention of gathering further information to support your developmental efforts.

Consider your preferred style of learning when incorporating varied resources into your learning program. Some people retain information best when it is presented in a multimedia format such as a videotape or interactive CD. Others learn best by reading technical manuals from a variety of different sources. Still others will gain most from the type of hands-on training that is provided by a workshop, seminar or course.

Use biblical principles to chart the development of your core competencies. There is no greater source of empowerment than the Word of God. Your ability to make the fundamental changes that are necessary for success is directly related to the amount of time and energy you spend meditating upon the life-giving principles of the Scriptures.

Step 3: Create a system to monitor your progress on an ongoing basis.

Schedule time in advance to assess your progress. Using the chart, specify the period of time when you will conduct "checkups" to evaluate and record your ongoing progress. Record the initial goal date, the intermediary goal date and the eventual date when you want to reach your final goal eliminating that weakness. You may want to use a simple rating scale (e.g., 1 through 10) to assess your progress, adding these ratings beside each date as you conduct your checkup. Use the journal lines below the chart to record more specific observations.

Developing Your Core Competencies

Use this chart to help you determine and develop your competencies and to overcome the weaknesses that hinder you from maximizing your competencies to fulfill your destiny.

Strengths	Priority Rating	Weaknesses	Priority Rating	Action Steps to Be Taken	Initial Goal	Mid Goal	Final Goal

My Progress Report

Use the lines below to journal your progress. You may want to record specific dates when you made important self-discovery about your actions or record the additional things you know you need to do to reach a final goal. Or you may merely want to journal how God's Word is helping you to reach your goals.

_____

_____

_____

Regardless of precisely how you go about it, regularly monitoring and recording of your progress will draw more attention to the tangible, though subtle, improvements that you experience throughout your development program. This information will serve as a reward and motivator. The process of ongoing self-monitoring also encourages the early identification of areas that will require more effort and/or time to develop than originally planned. This will allow you to modify your development plan proactively, rather than simply experiencing the demotivating frustration of failing to meet rigid target dates.

Ask others for input on your progress. Consider seeking the input of a mentor in the area in which you are seeking to develop new skills. Your mentor, a peer learning partner or a trusted colleague may have valuable suggestions that have worked for him or her in the past. Be willing to consider additional learning resources such as books, videos, workshops and the Internet for more perspectives on how to develop specific competencies (or aspects of competencies).

It is always a good idea to supplement self-monitoring with the feedback of others at all stages throughout a development plan. Record their observations along with yours, and pay extra attention to areas where their feedback does not correspond with your own self-monitoring. Find one or more learning partner(s) with whom you can provide mutual support, reinforcement, motivation and feedback. In identifying learning partners, considerations similar to those described above for a potential mentor would apply.

Establish timelines. Identify your final goal date for achieving each behavioral objective you have targeted. View the first goal dates and mid-goal dates as individual steps toward achieving the larger goal of developing an overall competency. Set realistic dates. Some dates may be relatively short-time spans, some may take longer, and some may require monitoring on an ongoing or long-term basis.

Prioritize targets. You may want to prioritize your targets so those you view as easiest to achieve and/or with the greatest payoff are implemented first. For example, "Hold weekly communications meetings" may be easier to implement than "Speak more eloquently" and may pay greater dividends.

Six Keys to Success in Your Development

Key 1. Assess yourself honestly.

A key to your success is the extent to which you are objective and honest in appraising your own strengths and weaknesses and targeting areas for improvement. Seeking further input from others is helpful, but it is important that you acknowledge and take responsibility for the areas that you can improve. The general rule of thumb in assessing yourself is this: Always be twice as hard on yourself as you are on others. Why? Because our nature is to overlook the "log" in our own eye while criticizing the "toothpick" in someone else's eye. By applying a greater measure of self-judgment, you will probably balance the scales between what you allow in yourself and what you despise in others.

Key 2. Capitalize on your strengths.

It is important to identify and develop your weaker competencies, but it is also important to identify and give attention to your areas of strength. Look for ways to increase your opportunities to exploit those strengths. Your overall effectiveness will be improved by making your strengths more prominent in your repertoire of skills and behaviors. You will also be able to rely on your strengths to compensate for your weaker areas while you work on eliminating these weaknesses. However, it is important that you do not allow yourself to fall back continually on your strengths to the exclusion of eliminating weaker areas.

Key 3. Set reasonable targets.

It is crucial that your learning plan target goals that are *doable* rather than lofty, over-optimistic long-term goals.

Reasonable goals will enable you to see more immediate and tangible progress. Recognizing the achievement associated with meeting those interim targets can serve as a source of reinforcement and motivation.

Key 4. Make a commitment.

It requires commitment and effort to eliminate your weakness and develop your competencies. For example, "creative people" do not necessarily generate innovative solutions and trend-setting ideas spontaneously. Many creative people view creativity as a skill that can be developed and exploited. They embrace methodologies or techniques that facilitate their creative process, and they actively exert the effort required to employ those methodologies. The amount of energy, time and resources you commit to learning will determine the success or failure of your personal development program.

Key 5. Believe that change is possible.

It is important that you understand and believe that change is both desirable and achievable. Cynicism or pessimism about a development plan will invariably become a self-fulfilling prophecy. It is a defining characteristic of humans that they undergo continuous transformation throughout their entire life span. When we stop changing we cease to be who we are. Change is inevitable; a learning plan simply ensures that the changes you undergo are targeted in a positive, constructive direction.

Key 6. Deny the right to be negative, and determine to be positive.

While it is important to be honest in assessing your weaknesses, it is equally important that you maintain a positive attitude toward yourself and your opportunities for success in your personal development efforts. Many people hold tightly to negative thoughts and crippling attitudes because they believe it is their "right" to wallow in self-pity. But winners always deny their flesh those false "rights" and intentionally choose to believe what the Word of God has to say about their identity and potential. Be aware of your strengths, and use them as leverage to assist you in developing your weaker areas.

Discovering the Cause

When young David discovered the giant Philistine Goliath intimidating the armies of Israel, he didn't set down with his laptop to type up a five-year vision for progressive change. He simply stood up and said, "Is there not a cause to destroy this uncircumcised covenant breaker?"[3] He was motivated by the power of a cause. A cause is a "motive or reason for human action."

A cause is always more powerful than a vision. I recently shared the platform with Pastor Bryan Houston of Hill Christian Centre, Sydney, Australia, in a South African leadership conference where he brought out some interesting thoughts concerning the power of a cause.[4] I have adapted a few of those principles for your consideration.

1. A vision is always personal, but a cause is corporate.

2. A vision can become outdated, but a cause will not change until it is fulfilled.

3. A vision can be possessed, but a cause will possess you.

4. People won't die for a vision, but they will for a cause.

5. A vision can be ignored, but a cause will confront you.

6. If you give yourself to the cause of the kingdom, God will honor your personal vision.

The apostle Paul is a classic example of a man who embraced the cause for which he was born. Though he was persecuted, rejected, misunderstood and falsely judged, he never once questioned the cause. It was forever settled in his mind. There comes a point in life when you have to settle the bottom line.

Some people struggle with their purpose because they've never clarified the cause! What is the cause for your life? Why were you born? Why were you created? Why were you brought into the kingdom of God?

I can give you the cause of Christianity—our corporate cause. It is to serve the King and the kingdom. We exist for the purpose of fulfilling the will of the King and accomplishing the purpose of the kingdom. But in the context of our corporate cause, what is your *individual* cause?

Developing Your Compassion

There will come a time after you have discovered your character, defined your core values, determined your competencies and discovered your cause when your compassion will create opportunities to advance you to the next level. Compassion empowers us to cross forbidden boundaries.

Remember the story of Mother Teresa? Compassion for one poverty-stricken, dying woman became the defining moment of her life. She decided to devote the rest of her life to easing the pain of those around her so they could live—or die—in dignity. Mother Teresa was once asked how she could continue day after day with visiting the terminally ill, feeding them, touching them, wiping their brows and giving them comfort as they lay dying. She replied, "It's not hard, because in each one I see the face of Christ in one of His more distressing disguises." On another occasion she said, "We have drugs for people with diseases like leprosy. But these drugs do not treat the main problem, the disease of being unwanted." Compassion took a young teacher in Calcutta to the next level as a human being, a servant of Christ and, ultimately, as a world leader.

The word *compassion* comes from two Latin words, *com* and *pati*, and literally means to "suffer with" others. Compassion, however, is more than mere sympathy—it is the combination of sympathy and action. Compassion is a driving force that empowers us to enter into suffering with others for the purpose of leading them into victory.

Determining the Power of Courage

Courage is a desperately needed commodity in this and every generation. In the weeks following the September 11, 2001 terrorist attack on America, we heard many heartwarming *and* heartbreaking stories of the heroes of the World Trade Center, the Pentagon and United Airlines Flight 93. Processing through the initial volume of human-interest stories that surfaced was no easy task, but a clear pattern of courage was undeniable. I found myself vacillating between sorrow and pride as the stories of sacrifice and selflessness began to emerge.

I wept as I read of the heroic actions of the Reverend Mychal Judge, a sixty-eight-year-old Franciscan priest who perished giving last rites to another victim at the World Trade Center. He lost his life while tending to the souls of the fallen. I smiled with pride at the story of the ex-Marine who saw the attack on television, walked out of the accounting firm where he worked, changed into his old uniform and rushed to ground zero in time to rescue two police officers. I marveled at the courage of the passengers of that ill-fated flight who refused to "go quietly into the night." Storming the terrorists, they brought the plane down in a remote field in Pennsylvania, saving countless lives and perhaps even the Capitol Building.

And there were the firefighters of Engine Company 28 and Ladder Company 11 who rushed into the flames of the burning towers and lost their lives saving others. They proved the words of G. K. Chesterton, who wrote, "Courage is almost a contradiction in terms. It means a strong desire to live, taking the form of a readiness to die."[5] Courage comes in many different forms and expresses itself in many unique ways, but every act of courage proceeds from a courageous life. The true basis for every form of courage is the courage *to be*. Our inner being determines the nature of our outer doing. Every act of courage is the expression of the courage to be.

One common thread runs through the lives of the heroes we study—they know who they are. Heroes rise to the challenge when difficulties and obstacles present themselves because their outer expression is the manifestation of their inner revelation. Their acts of courage come from an understanding of who they are.

Experiencing the Pleasure of God

The classic film *Chariots of Fire* won the Oscar in 1982 as the best movie of the year. It dramatized the story of two British runners, Eric Liddell and Harold Abrahams, who captured gold medals in the 1924 Olympics. Heavy underdogs, the pair triumphed through a remarkable display of character, discipline and courage. One scene in the film moved me in a profound way.

Liddell, an uncompromising Scottish Congregationalist, had been called by God to serve as a missionary in China at the conclusion of the international games. However, his deeply religious sister feared that if her brother won the gold, he would be so enamored with the fame and glory of an Olympic victory that he would opt out of his missionary vocation. On the eve of the race she pleaded fervently with him not to run. He looked at her with great affection and simply stated profound words that we will never forget: "But God made me fast, and when I run I feel His pleasure."

What a world of meaning in those powerful words! Moving to the next level is about the journey toward finding and fulfilling the pleasure of God. What are you doing that gives God pleasure? Are you continually "pressing toward the mark for the prize of the high calling of God in Christ Jesus"?[6]

Seeing Into Your Destiny

1. Write out the definition for success found in this chapter. Does the image fit your life?

2. Describe the three levels of personal emotional growth. On what level are you?

3. What is character? Can it be developed? If so, how?

4. List three differences between a cause and a vision.

5. In what activity do you experience the pleasure of God?

Profiles in Destiny

Profiles in Destiny

Throughout the course of World War II, the forces of Nazi Germany, led by Adolph Hitler, massacred over six million Jews in a sociopathic rage that shocked the rest of the world. In spite of the international outcry, most Germans were either indifferent or anti-Semitic, and few were daring enough to risk defying the wrath of Hitler's army. Oscar Schindler, however, chose to take a stand. His efforts resulted in the deliverance of twelve hundred Jews.

The movie *Schindler's List* reveals the heroic effort of this one man to outwit the Nazi regime. By purchasing a factory in Eastern Europe, Schindler was able to bribe German officials to allow him to use Jews as laborers for his business. Once these Jews were spared from the horrid conditions of the concentration camps, they were set free.

Toward the end of his life, the idea that he could have done more to save the Jews from genocide brought Oscar Schindler to the point of physical collapse. After risking his life and spending all of his wealth, he was not satisfied that he had done everything to rescue the innocent. In one poignant moment, his longtime assistant, Itzhak Stern, placed a gold ring in Schindler's hand. Schindler noticed an inscription on the ring.

"It's Hebrew," explained Stern. "It says, 'Whoever saves one life, saves the world.'"

Schindler put the ring onto his finger, nodded his thanks and then began to talk to himself: "I could've got more...if I'd just...I don't know, if I'd just...I could've got more."

In spite of his valiant effort and undeniable success, Schindler went to his grave feeling as if he could have saved just one more life. Such is the work of a world changer. It is never finished.

Chapter 11
Enjoying
the Journey

"Come to the edge," he said.
"We can't, Master, we're scared."
"Come to the edge," he said.
"We can't, Master, we're scared."
"Come to the edge," he said.
They came.
He pushed them…
They flew.

—Brandon Bays

I had always assumed I was fulfilling my assignment in life because, like many other overachievers, I was consumed with significant opportunities and important responsibilities. By the time I was thirty years old I had ministered in over fifty nations, founded and pastored two thriving churches, mentored hundreds of leaders and written several books. It wasn't until I reached my early thirties that I realized that I had confused *activity* with *destiny*. The foundation for that misunderstanding was laid in my childhood.

When I was four years old, my father graduated from Bible school and accepted an invitation from the home mission board of a classical Pentecostal denomination to plant a church in the Black Hills of South Dakota. He welcomed the opportunity, and we soon moved to a state we had never visited and a town whose name I could barely pronounce. The task would not be as easy as we had hoped. As a bivocational pastor, his days were spent providing for his family, and his nights were filled with ministry. Our family accepted the cost of doing the will of God without reservation or resistance. In spite of the hardships we encountered, we were happy to be working for God.

After ten long, hard years with little fruit to show for them, it was time to move again. This time we relocated to Louisiana to accept the pastorate of a small rural church. What a culture shock! Having spent the formative years of my childhood in the West, I felt as though we had been transferred to the foreign mission field. The sights, sounds and smells of the Deep South were mystifying to me, but I eventually settled in and learned to appreciate the opportunity we had been given. Two years later I graduated from high school and went off to Bible school.

By the time I founded my first church, I had spent almost two years in active ministry—and I was only eighteen years old! When the Lord directed me to plant a church in Kansas City, Missouri, I agreed on one condition: I would spend the rest of my life in one city, pastoring one congregation. As much as I appreciated the experiences of my childhood, I longed for the stability that comes with investing a lifetime into one vineyard.

Four years later I heard the same voice calling me to relocate to Tulsa, Oklahoma. I grudgingly responded and was soon involved in launching another growing congregation. God just didn't seem to be cooperating with my view of life and ministry.

A journey is like a marriage. The certain way to be wrong is to think you control it.

—*John Steinbeck*

The mid-1990s were a restless time for me. Everywhere I looked I was overwhelmed with the early warning signs of transition. The spiritual landscape of our congregation was shifting, a number of my primary relationships were changing, several of the programs that once worked were floundering, and God seemed to be hiding from my questions. The cloud was moving, and I wasn't quite sure where it was going or if I had the energy to follow.

Believing that my anxiety could be solved by simply revitalizing the same old wineskin, I gathered my resolve and attacked the problem aggressively. I put my roots down deeper into the soil of our community by purchasing land and entering into a multimillion-dollar building project. I studied the changing demographics of our congregation and community and developed new strategies for "inreach" and "outreach." I spent weeks in fasting and prayer. But in spite of my determination to succeed, the restlessness grew worse. As with Elijah of old, God was drying up my brook.

Finally, after an eleven-year run pastoring a dynamic congregation that had touched the lives of thousands of people in the region, I heard the same voice once again. God was calling me to start another church. For the first time in my life I said, "No way! I'm sorry, but I cannot do what You are asking me to do, Lord." Try as I would, I could not envision life in another city with another congregation. I had poured too much blood, sweat and tears into building the church, and this time I was determined to spend the rest of my life in one location.

My resistance was reinforced by idealism and the spiritual models I admired most. While many of my peers sought to emulate the latest, greatest televangelist of the moment, my childhood idols were always the veteran pastors who invested a lifetime into one community. In my mind, the principles of *fluidity* and *stability* were fundamentally opposed to one another. To live what I considered to be an unpredictable life following the will of God was a sure sign of instability. I longed for the permanence of my wife's family, whose father and grandfather founded and pastored the same congregation for fifty-six years. I was blind to the conflict that raged between my calling and my value system.

For three years I stifled the voice. Unlike Jonah, I refused to run from God; I simply stayed as close to Him as I could, all the while ignoring Him. I preached, prayed, praised and prophesied as loud as I could in a desperate attempt to drown out His voice, but He quietly insisted on having His way. My stubborn resistance began to affect my sense of well-being.

Many well-meaning friends attempted to counsel me during that three-year period of time with statements like: "Why would you even consider leaving a successful church, a great salary and a bright future in order to start another one?" Then of course there were numerous references to the ubiquitous midlife crisis. The problem with that one was my age! If what I was experiencing was a midlife crisis, then it must have been an extremely rare form of the early onset of juvenile midlife crisis.

You Listen Better While Lying Down

While climbing in the mountains of Southern Utah I experienced what seemed to be a minor heart attack. The whole frightening package was present—shortness of breath, numbness in my arms and an indescribable burst of pain in my chest. Being the stubborn individual that I am, I defied the doctor's orders, refusing to be admitted into the local hospital, and caught the first flight back to Tulsa. Judith met me at the airport gate, helped me into the car and rushed me to the emergency room. Within one hour of landing I was wheeled into the intensive care unit of St. Francis Hospital connected to IVs, oxygen and a heart monitor, fighting for every breath. The chest pain returned with a vengeance.

The next ten days were a blur as I submitted to a battery of tests. I was probed and inspected in places that I still can't describe without blushing. When the doctors couldn't locate the source of the chest pain, they finally called in a specialist from the Mayo Clinic, who soon discovered the problem.

"Mr. Crist," he began "in fifteen years of practice I have never seen what I witnessed today."

Swallowing hard to push back the fear, I managed to croak, "What was it?"

"Your stomach contains at least a hundred ulcers, and that

may even be a conservative estimate. While you were unconscious, I took a color picture of 10 percent of your stomach, and it reveals a dozen deeply lacerated ulcers."

I was too stunned to reply.

"Along with that discovery, I've also diagnosed you as having an upper esophageal spasm. When the spasm triggers, it registers against the wall of your heart and appears to be a heart attack. But it isn't.

"By the way, Mr. Crist," he concluded, "have you been under any stress the past few months? You sure look like it."

By then I had regained my voice, but not my composure. I wanted to shout, "Whata ya' mean, the past few months? I've been under stress for about three years now! It all began when God began to speak to me about moving. Get Him to back off, and I'm sure the stress will go away!"

My recovery began the following day when my wife walked into the hospital room with my schedule in one hand and a red pen in the other. "We're changing the way we live," she boldly announced. "From now on we're going to simplify life and do what really matters."

I glared at her with the look I've long reserved for my mortician. "What do you mean...simplify? I have places to go, people to see and projects to complete. I don't have any time for simplification." The sarcasm dripped from my tongue like acid from a cracked battery cell. But as much as I wanted to deny it, I knew she was right.

During the following months I began to understand finally what God was really saying to me. I had fallen into the performance trap and was working harder than ever—only to frustrate the grace of God in the process. I wanted God to give me just enough space to have my own way. But I didn't want Him to be too far away to rescue me when I needed help. Like many other Christian leaders, I had subconsciously accepted the idea that God is only needed in times of crisis or when we're in need of the miraculous. After all, as long as we can do the work, why bother Him? Out of my stubborn independence, I was *doing* myself to death instead of simply *being* who He created me to be. It's remarkable what you can learn when you are lying flat on your back.

A journey of a thousand miles begins with a single step.

—*Chinese Proverb*

A Long Journey in the Right Direction

Tucked away in our subconscious mind is an idyllic vision we have for the future. We live as if we were traveling by train, and from the window we view life as if it were being lived by those we pass by. Along the way we catch meaningful glimpses of parents, children, friends and neighbors, along with the fleeting images of our calling and purpose in life. Nevertheless, uppermost in our minds is the final destination toward which we are racing—the station that will provide the fulfillment for which we are longing. We will, we assure ourselves, eventually arrive at the station.

When that day finally arrives, so many wonderful dreams will come true. So we restlessly pace the aisles and count the miles, peering ahead, waiting for the final destination. Eventually we realize there is no station in this life, no earthly place at which to arrive. In his brilliant essay titled "The Station," Robert Hasting explains, "The true joy of life is the trip. The station is only a dream. It constantly outdistances us." He continues, "It isn't the burden of today that drives men mad. It is the regret over yesterday and the fear of tomorrow. Regret and fear are twin thieves who rob us of today. So stop pacing the aisles and counting the miles. Instead climb more mountains, eat more ice cream, go barefoot more often, swim more rivers, watch more sunsets, laugh more, cry less. Life must be lived as we go along. The station will come soon enough."[1]

Don't be so consumed with where you are going that you miss where you presently are.

What does that mean? It means that while striving for success we can miss the enjoyment of the successes we have already accomplished. We work so hard to be whoever we are destined to be that we are miss out on the exciting journey. The secret to living a joyful and peaceful life is in learning to enjoy the journey.

The Joy Is in the Journey

As I began the process of sifting through the layers of thirty years of performance-oriented Christianity, I discovered that my attempts to work *for* God were the humanist counterpart to God's desire to work *with* me. My *doing* had overshadowed my *being* until finally I was reduced to the level of a human marionette. Religion was the puppet master, and I was dancing on command. I was striving to earn what I had been freely given. Like Rip Van Winkle waking up from a twenty-year nap, I suddenly saw how much of life I had missed. I was created to be loved. I was created to be accepted. *I was created to be fathered. And I was created to enjoy the journey.*

And so were you.

After repenting of my rotten attitude and reorienting my perspective, I realized that the call to relocate was not some form of divine punishment. God was giving me the opportunity to journey with Him in His mission to fill all the earth with His glory.[2] As I embraced the calling on my life, my joy returned. And as my joy returned my health was restored. Ninety days later I submitted to another battery of tests and was pronounced ulcer free. My doctors are still scratching their heads.

Shortly after moving to Scottsdale, Arizona, to launch CitiChurch International, I revised our ministry vision statement to reflect the new values that were established in my life through this process of discovery. Our ministry vision statement now reads: "Our vision is to influence our generation through loving, laughing and living under the lordship of Jesus Christ. We believe that life was designed to be lived, people were created to be loved, laughter heals the soul and our lives always work best when submitted to the lordship of Jesus Christ."[3]

Through the process of rediscovering my purpose in life I have come to the conclusion that there is nothing as tragic as being alive and not enjoying life. I wasted far too many years because I didn't know how to enjoy where I was on the way to where I am going.

Packing for the Journey

Have you ever taken an extended journey? Did you pack enough belongings for the entire trip? Nothing can be more frustrating than to be stuck in a foreign environment without the essentials of life. I believe packing (naturally, spiritually and emotionally) is a skill that can only be learned through the process of trial and error. As we learn our way through life, we should consistently assess what attitudes, emotions, aspirations and apparel are appropriate in the different situations we encounter.

Traveling as I do as a conference and seminar speaker, I have logged over a million miles on one airline alone! Through the process of trial and error I have discovered two things: Each trip should be properly considered in advance, and I am the only one responsible for what is placed (or not placed) in my suitcase. I missed both of these important principles in my early years of traveling and ended up wearing the wrong color socks and the wrong attitude in a number of situations in which I found myself.

Here are some of the important skill sets, attitudes and belongings you will want to pack for the journey.

Your Trip Essentials

❏ Flexibility	❏ Adaptability	❏ Resilience
❏ Humility	❏ Discipline	❏ Self-control
❏ Joy	❏ Gratitude	❏ Family
❏ Friends	❏ Mentors	❏ Leaders
❏ Perseverance	❏ Focus	❏ Vision
❏ Commitment	❏ Grace	❏ Cheerfulness
❏ Forgiveness	❏ Tolerance	❏ _____

There Is Abundance in the Journey

When describing His journey in life, Jesus said, "I have come that they may have life, and that they may have it more abundantly."[4] The word *abundant* is the Greek *ekperissos*, which literally means "superabundance." This is not even your average, well-balanced, moderate measure of abundance. This is abundance beyond measure.

Now if that wasn't enough, Jesus also used another superlative when He threw in the Greek word translated *more*. To paraphrase, Jesus actually said, "I have come that you might have life *more* superabundant." Jesus is compounding phrases and using multiple superlatives in a single sentence to describe just how extreme this kind of life is. He came to bring us a *redundant* measure of abundance.

Listen to the words of Paul to the Ephesians: "Now to Him who is able to do *exceedingly abundantly* above all that we ask or think, according to the power that works in us."[5] Here we go again. This word "abundantly" is the same one Jesus used when describing His mission in life. It is *ekperissos*, which literally means *superabundance*. And like Jesus, Paul is not satisfied in using the strongest form of the word, so he throws in "exceedingly"! The word *exceedingly* is the Greek word *huper*, from which we get the word *hyper*. It means "over, above, beyond, superior to, more than." Paul is describing *hyper superabundance*. This is an incomprehensible measure. Wow!

The life that Jesus offers us is the kind of life that is greater in degree than superabundance. It is redundant abundance. You may be thinking, *I find that hard to believe. My life is anything but abundant. What do I have so abundant?*

John 15 reveals six things that each of us possesses.

1. You have an abundance of truth.[6]

2. You have an abundance of love.[7]

3. You have an abundance of joy.[8]

4. You have an abundance of purpose.[9]

5. You have an abundance of opportunities.[10]

6. You have an abundance of spiritual help.[11]

God has not left you to struggle with insufficiency on your journey. These building blocks of abundance can become the foundation for a life of superabundance. If you believe the truth, walk in love, take strength from joy, pursue your purpose, take advantage of every opportunity and rely on the Holy Spirit, you will build a foundation of superabundance. There is super-abundance in the journey.

> **He who postpones the hour of living rightly is like the rustic who waits for the river to run out before he crosses.**
>
> —*Horace*

It's Never Too Late to Begin

When the late Nadine Stair, of Louisville, Kentucky, was eighty-five years old, she was asked what she would do if she had her life to live over again. "I'd make more mistakes next time," she said. "I'd relax. I would limber up. I would be sillier than I have been this trip. I would take fewer things seriously. I would take more chances. I would climb more mountains and swim more rivers. I would eat more ice cream and less beans. I would perhaps have more actual troubles, but I'd have fewer imaginary ones. You see, I'm one of those people who live sensibly and sanely hour after hour, day after day. Oh, I've had my moments, and if I had to do it over again, I'd have more of them. In fact, I'd try to have nothing else. Just moments, one after another, instead of living so many years ahead of each day. I've been one of those persons who never go anywhere without a thermometer, a hot water bottle and a raincoat. If I had to do it over again, I would travel lighter than I have. If I had my life to live over, I would start barefoot earlier in the spring and stay that way later in the fall. I would go to more dances. I would ride more merry-go-rounds. I would pick more daisies."[12]

Nadine addresses a way of life we all struggle with at some point. There are two equal and opposite forces that act on us all the time. One force says, "You haven't given enough. Work hard. Push harder. You can always sleep when you die."

The other voice simply says, "Slow down and enjoy the process." The voice to which we listen determines where we end up when our journey is completed.

You see, in life we must realize that the joy doesn't just come from the journey—it comes from *enjoying the journey*. Take time out for you, take time out for your family and friends, and take time out to enjoy the passion that lives within you. If you take the necessary time that you need to enjoy the journey, the success will mean so much more in the end.

There are many problems that we can face each day. But even if our circumstances are not what we desire, let's make a quality decision to make the most of every moment while we're heading toward where we want to be.

You can awaken to destiny and fulfill everything God has designed for you to accomplish.

Seeing Into Your Destiny

1. What have you accomplished in life that still brings you joy?

2. What is it you wish you could enjoy more of?

3. Who are the people in your life who have suffered the most? (Don't be surprised if it comes down to the answer being you.)

4. What do you need to pack for the next leg of your journey?

5. Take a sheet of paper and list the six things that you have in abundance. Commit them to memory.

NOTES

Introduction: Destined for an Awakening

1. Anne Tyler, *The Accidental Tourist* (New York: Berkley Publishing Group, 1994).
2. Philippians 1:6

Chapter One: Confessions of a Recovering Sleepwalker

1. William Faulkner once said, "The best stories are the ones we're most ashamed of." Dad, just be thankful that we don't have any worse skeletons in the family closet!
2. Ephesians 1:18
3. Ephesians 2:1, 5; Colossians 2:13
4. Ephesians 4:18
5. Mark 8:22–25
6. Philippians 3:15, The Message
7. Oliver Sacks, M.D., *Awakenings* (Mangolia, MA: Peter Smith Pub., 1990).
8. Colossians 3:1–4
9. Romans 13:11
10. Revelation 6:10; 13:14; 14:6; 17:8
11. Philippians 3:19
12. James 1:17
13. Ephesians 2:6
14. Taken from live satellite seminar, *Worldwide Lessons in Leadership*, 1996, sponsored by the University of Tulsa, Tulsa, OK.
15. *The Columbia World of Quotations* (New York: Columbia University Press, 1996), s.v. 60434, "Economy" (1854).

Chapter Two: The God Who Awakens Men

1. Proverbs 8:17
2. Jeremiah 29:13
3. Matthew 26:36–44, The Message
4. Arthur W. Pink, *The Sovereignty of God* (Grand Rapids, MI: Baker Books, 1969), 263.
5. Merrill F. Unger, *Unger's Bible Dictionary*, (Chicago: Moody Press, 1957,1961, 1966), s.v. "sovereignty of God."
6. Acts 4:24, NIV
7. *Westminster Confession of Faith*, Westminster Shorter Catechism
8. Acts 13:36
9. Psalm 139:16, NIV
10. Romans 9:17–24

11. Proverbs 21:1
12. George F. Santa, *A Modern Study The Book of Proverbs: Charles Bridges' Classic Revised for Today's Reader* (Milford, MI: Mott Media, 1978), 432.
13. Genesis 37–45
14. Daniel 4:35
15. James 4:13–16
16. Proverbs 19:21, NIV
17. J. B. Phillips, *Your God Is Too Small,* reprint edition (New York: Scribner, 1997).
18. Hebrews 13:8
19. Steven Ashly, "Smart Cars and Automated Highways," *Mechanical Engineering* (May 1998). Article obtained from Internet, www.memagazine.org/backissues/may98/features/smarter/smarter.html.
20. Proverbs 3:5–6
21. Robert Burns, "To a Mouse, On Turning Up Her Nest With the Plough," November 1785.

CHAPTER THREE: PREDESTINED TO BE AWAKENED

1. Norman Geisler, *Chosen But Free* (Minneapolis, MN: Bethany House Publishers, 1999), 42.
2. Westminster Catechism, emphasis added.
3. Ephesians 1:11
4. James 1:13–15
5. This is the general conclusion of a book by Franky Schaeffer titled *A Time for Anger: The Myth of Neutrality* (Wheaton, IL: Good News Publishers, 1982).
6. Martin Luther, *The Bondage of the Will*, section 26, 1525.
7. Ibid.
8. "Gotta Serve Somebody" by Bob Dylan. Copyright © 1979 by Special Rider Music. All rights reserved. International copyright secured. Reprinted by permission.
9. Galatians 5:1
10. Proverbs 29:18, KJV
11. Colossians 1:1, 6, 10, THE MESSAGE
12. Stephen Covey, *First Things First: To Live, to Love, to Learn, to Leave a Legacy* (New York: Fireside, 1996), 103.
13. Job 2:10
14. Psalm 47:4
15. Source obtained from the Internet: "Three Principles of Discipleship (Part 2)," www.exchangedlife.com/sermons/topical/discip-2.shtml.

16. Terry Crist, *The Image Maker* (Lake Mary, FL: Charisma House, 2000), 57.

CHAPTER FOUR: HISTORY BELONGS TO THE AWAKENED

1. William Raymond Manchester, *Winston Churchill: The Last Lion: Alone 1932-1940* (New York: Delta, 1988), 674.
2. Hyrum W. Smith, *What Matters Most* (New York: Simon and Schuster, 2000), 33.
3. See Romans 12:6.
4. Psalm 37:23
5. "The Story of Flight 93," *Dateline NBC*, aired October 2, 2001.
6. Matthew 26:9, 13
7. Mark 15:42–47
8. Max Dupree, *Leadership Is an Art* (New York: Doubleday, 1989).
9. Luke 14:25–33
10. Leighton Ford, *Transforming Leadership* (Westmont, IL: Intervarsity Press, 1993).
11. Graham Nown, *The World's Worst Predictions* (London: Arrow, 1985).
12. Romans 4:17, emphasis added
13. Hebrews 11:1–3
14. Hebrews 11:7–8
15. Matthew 6:10
16. Genesis 1:27
17. Joshua 17:15, 18; 1 Samuel 2:29; Ezekiel 21:19a, b; 23:47
18. Ezekiel 21:19, KJV. The verb *choose* is the Hebrew transliterated *bara*, which means "to create, shape, form." Ezekiel was also commanded to prophesy to the dry bones of the massacred army in Ezekiel 37. His words were the prophetic catalyst for the creative power of God to manifest. Creativity has its origin in God, and we are allowed to partner with Him for its emergence.
19. Genesis 1:28
20. Genesis 2:15
21. I heard Guy Chevreau make this statement at a leadership conference at Toronto Airport Christian Fellowship, Toronto, Canada, in the winter of 1996.

CHAPTER FIVE: YOUR IDENTITY IS YOUR DESTINY

1. Author's paraphrase of 1 John 4:20
2. Psalm 139:14
3. Genesis 1:26
4. A quote from Herman Bavinck, as quoted in Anthony Hoekema,

Created in God's Image (Grand Rapids, MI: Wm. B. Eerdman's Publishing, 1994), 3:137.

5. Crist, *The Image Maker,* 30.

6. Acts 17:28

7. James 3:11–12

8. Taken from a sermon titled "Building a Life of Purpose," by Dr. Darryl Dash, December 12, 2000. Tape available by contacting Richview Baptist Church, 1548 Kipling Avenue, Toronto, Ontario, Canada M9R 4A3.

9. Eric Hoffer, *Reflections on the Human Condition* (New York: HarperCollins, 1973).

10. Ravi Zacharias, "Shepherding a Soul-Less Culture," *Just Thinking* (Spring/Summer 1999): 2.

11. Source obtained from the Internet: Taken from www.sermonillustrations.com.

12. Myles Munroe, *Understanding Your Potential* (Shippensburg, PA: Destiny Image Publishers, 1991), 23.

13. Romans 9:21

14. Matthew 25:24–25

15. 2 Corinthians 5:16

CHAPTER SIX: FINDING THE COURAGE TO BE

1. Quoted in John C. Maxwell, *The Success Journey* (Nashville, TN: Thomas Nelson Publishers, 1997), 121.

2. Ibid.

3. Ibid.

4. Anne Wilson Schaef, *When Society Becomes an Addict* (San Francisco, CA: HarperSanFrancisco, 1988).

5. Hebrews 2:14

6. 2 Timothy 1:7

7. John 1:12

8. Job 3:8; 41:1; Psalm 104:26; Isaiah 27:1

9. Psalm 89:10; Isaiah 51:9

10. Matthew 14:28, author's paraphrase

11. This concept opened up to me while listening to Michael Slaughter teach on being "Fully Human." The tape can be ordered from Ginghamsburg Resources, 6759 South County Road 25A, Tipp City, Ohio 45371.

12. Acts 20:28

13. Matthew 5:44

14. Exodus 4:2

15. Matthew 16:17–18

16. Luke 22:31
17. Matthew 26:34
18. Jeremiah 17:9
19. Philippians 1:6
20. Soren Kierkegaard, "Irony as a Mastered Moment: The Truth of Irony, The Concept of Irony," part 2, 1841, translated 1966.
21. Matthew 25:14–30

CHAPTER SEVEN: BORN TO RULE—TRAINED TO REIGN

1. Galatians 3:29
2. Romans 8:14, emphasis added
3. Jesus spoke of Himself metaphorically as the door in Luke 11:9; 13:24.
4. Galatians 4:1–2, NIV
5. Numbers 34:2
6. Numbers 33:53–54
7. 1 Samuel 12:16
8. Ephesians 1:18
9. Revelation 13:8
10. Jeremiah 29:11
11. Ephesians 4:7
12. 2 Peter 1:3
13. 1 Corinthians 1:30
14. Acts 1:8
15. Proverbs 17:6
16. 3 John 2
17. Psalm 5:12
18. Proverbs 16:7
19. Matthew 5:5
20. Genesis 1:27–28
21. Genesis 37:3
22. Genesis 45:4–5
23. Hebrews 5:8
24. Romans 5:17
25. 1 Peter 5:7
26. Matthew 20:16
27. Alan E. Nelson, *Embracing Brokenness* (Colorado Springs, CO: NavPress, 2002), 18
28. Matthew 21:44
29. Matthew 6:10, KJV
30. Romans 12:1–2
31. Ephesians 6:8

32. Hebrews 6:12
33. Habakkuk 2:2

Chapter Eight: Life Designs

1. Ray R. Sutton, *That You May Prosper* (Tyler, TX: Institute for Christian Economics, 1987).
2. Psalm 24:1, emphasis added
3. John Pollock, *Wilberforce* (Herts and Belleville, MI: Lion, 1977), 37–39.
4. Proverbs 22:6, emphasis added
5. Anthony Robbins, *Unlimited Power* (New York, NY: Fawcett Columbine, 1986), 343.
6. Crist, *The Image Maker*, 131.
7. Romans 12:1–2
8. 2 Corinthians 10:3–5
9. James 1:22
10. Deuteronomy 16:3

Chapter Nine: Moving From Disappointment to Destiny

1. Brian Tracy, "The Psychology of Achievement," an audiocassette series published by the Nightingale-Conant Corporation in 1989.
2. Quoted by John C. Maxwell, *Failing Forward* (Nashville, TN: Thomas Nelson Publishers, 2000), 115.
3. Ibid., 92.
4. 1 Corinthians 2:9
5. 2 Corinthians 12:7–8
6. My thanks to the anonymous public speaker who first coined this acronym. This author has benefited from your creativity.
7. Inspired by John C. Maxwell's book *Falling Forward* (Nashville: Thomas Nelson, 2000).
8. 1 Samuel 17:26
9. Matthew 4:19
10. Matthew 3:17
11. Acts 10:34, KJV
12. Matthew 20:1–15, author's paraphrase
13. Psalm 47:4
14. 2 Timothy 4:10
15. Philippians 3:3
16. Jeremiah 17:5
17. Friedrich Nietzcshe, *Sämtliche Werke: Kritische Studienausgabe*, vol. 2, eds. Giorgio Colli and Mazzino Montinari (Berline: de Gruyter, 1980), 642. *The Wanderer and His Shadow*, aphorism 206,

"Forgetting Our Objectives" (1880).

18. Source obtained from the Internet: www.sportsillustrated.com and www.lancearmstrong.com.

CHAPTER TEN: LIVING AT THE NEXT LEVEL

1. Stephen Covey, *Principle-Centered Leadership* (New York: Simon and Schuster, 1992).
2. This concept was adapted from Sue Mallory and Brad Smith, *The Equipping Church Guidebook* (Grand Rapids, MI: Zondervan, 2001), 241.
3. 1 Samuel 17:26
4. The cassette tape of Bryan Houston speaking in a South African leadership conference is available through His People Christian Ministries, The Louis Group Building, first floor, 2 Boundary Road, Century City, 7441, Cape Town, RSA.
5. G. K. Chesterton, *Orthodoxy* (Wheaton, IL: Harold Shaw Publishers, 2001), Chapter 6. (Original publication date, 1909.)
6. Philippians 3:14, KJV

CHAPTER ELEVEN: ENJOYING THE JOURNEY

1. Robert Hasting, "The Station," as quoted in Brandon Bays, *The Journey* (New York: Pocket Books, 1999), viii.
2. Psalm 72:19
3. Vision statement from CitiChurch International, Scottsdale, Arizona. Catalog of leadership training materials available upon request from Citichurch, P.O. Box 14553, Scottsdale, AZ 85267 or from www.citichurch.com.
4. John 10:10
5. Ephesians 3:20, emphasis added
6. John 15:7
7. John 15:9
8. John 15:11
9. John 15:16
10. John 15:16
11. John 15:26
12. This story has become somewhat of an urban legend, and has been used by Richard Bolles, Jack Canfield and Anthony Robbins. It was first published in *Family Circle*, vol. 91, no. 4 (March 27, 1978): 99.

Terry Crist has other books and audio and video products available. To obtain a catalog or to request more information about his church, apostolic network or ministry, please contact:

Terry Crist
SpiritBuilder Seminars and Resources
P.O. Box 14553
Scottsdale, AZ 85267

(480) 661-9209

Visit his website at www.terrycrist.com

For more information concerning this book, visit www.awakenedtodestiny.com

If you enjoyed Awakened to Destiny, *here are some other titles from Charisma House that we think will minister to you . . .*

The Image Maker
Terry Crist
ISBN: 0-88419-637-2
Retail Price: $12.99

How many of us know just how special we are to God? Terry Crist says that when we were born again, our spiritual DNA was recoded. A profound change took place. As we begin to know—in our deepest being—who we are in Him, we can move into the flow of God's anointing and power.

Nevertheless
Mark Rutland
ISBN: 0-88419-847-2
Retail Price: $9.99

With one unassuming word, Jesus freed us and revealed the love of God. Jesus captured the awesome power of this word in the Garden of Gethsemane. Jesus prayed, and heaven and earth rejoiced. If you want to confuse the enemy—say *Nevertheless*. Should terrible events threaten to overwhelm you and rip at the foundations of your soul, remember you still have an answer . . . *Nevertheless*.

The Priestly Bride
Anna Rountree
ISBN: 0-88419-766-2
Retail Price: $13.99

The Priestly Bride contains a revelation that was given to the author and includes awesome insights into the processes of purification and sanctification that will take readers right to the heart of God. Within these pages is a spiritual quest into intense and dynamic levels of intimacy between the Bridegroom and His bride.

Charisma® HOUSE
Books about Spirit-Led Living

To pick up a copy of any of these titles, contact your local Christian bookstore or order online at www.charismawarehouse.com.